To the memory of my father
William John Niven, Sr.

John Niven
THE CLAREMONT GRADUATE SCHOOL

The Coming
of the
Civil War

1837–1861

HARLAN DAVIDSON, INC.
WHEELING, ILLINOIS 60090-6000

Library of Congress Cataloging-in-Publication Data

Niven, John.
  The coming of the Civil War, 1837–1861
  p.   cm. — (The American history series)
  Includes bibliographical references.
  1. United States—History—1815-1861.   2. United States—
History—Civil War, 1861–1865—Causes.   I. Title.   II. Series:
American history series (Wheeling, Ill.)
E415.7.N54   1990
973.5—dc20   89-23531
ISBN 0-88295-861-5

Cover design: Roger Eggers. Cover illustration: "The Bombard-ment of Fort Sumter by the Batteries of the Confederate States, April 13, 1861." Originally published in *Harper's Weekly*, 1861.

Manufactured in the United States of America
99 98 97 96 EB 3 4 5

The American History Series

SERIES EDITORS
John Hope Franklin, *Duke University*
Abraham S. Eisenstadt, *Brooklyn College*

Arthur S. Link
GENERAL EDITOR FOR HISTORY

FOREWORD

Every generation writes its own history, for the reason that it sees the past in the foreshortened perspective of its own experience. This has certainly been true of the writing of American history. The practical aim of our historiography is to offer us a more certain sense of where we are going by helping us understand the road we took in getting where we are. If the substance and nature of our historical writing is changing, it is precisely because our own generation is redefining its direction, much as the generation that preceded us redefined theirs. We are seeking a newer direction, because we are facing new problems, changing our values and premises, and shaping new institutions to meet new needs. Thus, the vitality of the present inspires the vitality of our writing about our past. Today's scholars are hard at work reconsidering every major field of our history: its politics, diplomacy, economy, society, mores, values, sexuality, and status, ethnic, and race relations. No less significantly, our scholars are using newer modes of investigation to probe the ever-expanding domain of the American past.

Our aim, in this American History Series, is to offer the reader a survey of what scholars are saying about the central themes and issues of American history. To present these themes and issues, we have invited scholars who have made notable contributions to the respective fields in which they are writing. Each volume offers the reader a sufficient factual and narrative account for perceiving the larger dimensions of its particular subject. Addressing their respective themes, our authors have undertaken, moreover, to present the conclusions derived by the principal writers on these themes. Beyond that, the authors present their own conclusions about those aspects of their respective subjects that have been matters of difference and controversy. In effect, they have written not only about where the subject stands in today's historiography but also about where they stand on their subject. Each volume closes with an extensive critical essay on the writings of the major authorities on its particular theme.

The books in this series are designed for use in both basic and advanced courses in American history. Such a series has a particular utility in times such as these, when the traditional format of our American history courses is being altered to accommodate a greater diversity of texts and reading materials. The series offers a number of distinct advantages. It extends and deepens the dimensions of course work in American history. In proceeding beyond the confines of the traditional textbook, it makes clear that the study of our past is, more than the student might otherwise infer, at once complex, sophisticated, and profound. It presents American history as a subject of continuing vitality and fresh investigation. The work of experts in their respective fields, it opens up to the student the rich findings of historical inquiry. It invites the student to join, in major fields of research, the many groups of scholars who are pondering anew the central themes and problems of our past. It challenges the student to participate actively in exploring American history and to collaborate in the creative and rigorous adventure of seeking out its wider reaches.

John Hope Franklin
Abraham S. Eisenstadt

CONTENTS

Foreword / vii
Preface / xi
Chronology of Events / xiii

INTRODUCTION / 1

Genesis of Colonial Slavery / 2
The Constitutional Debate on Slavery / 5
Regional Development and New Discord / 7
Impact of Reform / 13

CHAPTER ONE: **Tensions** / 18

Abolitionism and National Politics / 19
Emerging Sectionalism / 22
States' Rights: Theory and Practice / 26
Depression and the Second American Party System / 29
Southern Fears / 34
The High Tide of Reform / 37

CHAPTER TWO: **A Temporary Armistice** / 45

Tippecanoe, Tyler, and Texas / 46
Expansion and War with Mexico / 49
Stalemate / 54
California and Compromise / 58
A Prophetic Statement / 64

x Contents

Chapter Three: **Kansas, First Phase** / 69

  Whig Disintegration / 71
  Young America / 74
  The Kansas-Nebraska Bill / 79
  Birth of the Republican Party / 85
  Bleeding Kansas / 87

Chapter Four: **Disruption** / 96

  The Election of 1856 / 97
  Dred Scott / 99
  Kansas, Second Phase / 104
  Lincoln and Douglas / 109
  John Brown's Raid on Harpers Ferry / 113
  Panic and Political Paralysis / 115

Chapter Five: **Disunion** / 121

  The Election of 1860 / 121
  The Lower South Secedes / 130
  Buchanan and the National Crisis / 131
  War Begins / 137

  Bibliographical Explanations / 144
  Index / 175

Maps

  The United States in 1850 / 44
  The Kansas-Nebraska Act, 1854 / 68
  The Election of 1860 / 120

PREFACE

On a pleasant afternoon in Charleston, South Carolina, at the annual meeting of the Southern Historical Association, Harlan Davidson called me aside and asked me if I would fill in a gap in the American History Series by writing on the coming of the Civil War. Harlan had read and liked my biography of Martin Van Buren that had just been published. He proposed that I do a book that would deal specifically with the period between Van Buren's administration and the outbreak of the Civil War, a time span of twenty-four years during which the Union gradually fragmented under what seemed to be unbearable social and economic pressures.

After some hesitation I agreed to take on the task. The reason for my brief indecision was an unusual accumulation of work that had to be completed before I could begin a new project. Harlan and his successors, Angela Davidson and Maureen Gilgore Hewitt, were most understanding when I missed several deadlines. And I am most grateful to him and to those who have carried on his high-minded philosophy of publishing. But I am also grateful for the careful and creative guidance I received from the editors of this series, John Hope Franklin and Abraham Eisenstadt. Under their tutelage the manuscript grew in breadth and depth. I had the benefit of advice from five colleagues, ripe scholars all, who read the manuscript in its early stages. They are Robert V. Remini,

Henry Gibbons, William M. Evans, Charles Lofgren, and John H. Kemble. I reserve a special note of appreciation to J. Michael Kendrick, assistant editor at Harlan Davidson, Inc., for his careful and creative editing in the final phases of publication. But I must emphasize that I bear sole responsibility for interpretation and for any errors or omissions. Finally I would like to thank Lelah Mullican, who typed and retyped the manuscript.

John Niven

CHRONOLOGY OF EVENTS

1837 Van Buren elected President; Panic of 1837
1839 Liberty party formed
1840 Whig candidate W. H. Harrison wins presidential election
1844 Polk elected President
1845 Texas admitted to the Union
1846 Mexican-American War begins; Wilmot Proviso introduced in House
1848 Treaty of Guadalupe Hidalgo ends war with Mexico; Free Soil party formed; Zachary Taylor wins election of 1848
1850 Admission of California as free state; Compromise of 1850; Nashville Convention; Calhoun dies
1852 *Uncle Tom's Cabin* published; Pierce defeats Scott in presidential election
1853 Gadsden Purchase completes continental United States
1854 Kansas-Nebraska bill passed; Ostend Manifesto issued in Brussels; Republican party organized
1856 Buchanan defeats Frémont, first Republican presidential candidate; "Bleeding Kansas"; Charles Sumner attacked in Senate
1857 Dred Scott decision; economic panic
1858 Douglas breaks with Buchanan over Lecompton constitution; Lincoln-Douglas debates

1859   John Brown raids Harpers Ferry; scandals in Buchanan cabinet

1860   Democratic party splits at Charleston convention; Lincoln wins presidential election; South Carolina secedes

1861   Confederacy formed; Fort Sumter attacked; Civil War begins

INTRODUCTION

"The Government had an air of social instability and incompleteness that went far to support the right of secession in theory as in fact, but right or wrong, secession was likely to be easy where there was so little to secede from. The Union was a sentiment, but not much more." So wrote Henry Adams about the winter of 1860–61 in Washington, D.C., many years after the events he described as an eyewitness had transpired. His comment, tinged with irony and the air of impudence that so often characterizes his writing, provides us with an important clue in our efforts to understand the roots of the conflict that was about to rend the nation. Adams was a close if sardonic observer. A highly educated Bostonian, he wrote from a perspective which did not regard the Union in the same way as a midwesterner might, a person like Abraham Lincoln for example, whose heritage was bound up with the expansion of the Union, not with the aristocratic, two-hundred-year-old legacy of a Bay State family. Yet even with his background and the obvious distortions that occur when memory is refracted through the lens of time, Adams's remarks about the nature of the Union must be taken seriously.

The federal government that was created in 1789 was built on a series of compromises that were made to satisfy political, social, and economic conditions as they existed at that time. James Madison, a member of the Philadelphia Convention from Virginia, saw more clearly than most of his fellow delegates the problems involved in reconciling all the diverse interests and particularist loyalties of the several states with the overarching entity of a federal union. Thus he devised and promoted the idea of "a middle ground" between national and state power. In the main, Madison and his supporters succeeded in persuading the convention to accept a division of sovereignty in which a portion of power was entrusted to the national government and the remainder to the states and the people. In doing so they left important issues of governance open to future interpretation. Almost immediately the powers of the new government to act through its representative body, the Congress, collided with the reserved powers of the states. Madison sided with Thomas Jefferson in favoring a greater role for states' rights in contrast to Alexander Hamilton's centralist ideas for a strong national government. Subsequently, political doctrine evolved through searching debate and judicial interpretation that reinforced both philosophies of government. Indeed for the first seventy years of constitutional government the nature of the Union was the prime object of political discussion as politicians and statesmen sought to define its meaning and how it shaped the outlines of the nation's future.

Genesis of Colonial Slavery

A particularly thorny controversy that would eventually defy any solution short of violent means was the institution of slavery. Ever since 1619, when a Dutch trading vessel brought in blacks who were sold to the tobacco planters around Jamestown, Virginia, slavery gradually rooted itself in the American South. It grew slowly in the Virginia colony during the seventeenth century but within the next hundred years rapidly expanded into neighboring regions. Blacks were deemed hardier and better able than whites to withstand the humid, malarial conditions of these areas, where cash crops such as sugar, tobacco, rice, and indigo for dye were raised for export. But equally important in these early stages of growth, as Edmund Morgan has shown in his *American Slavery, American Freedom: The Ordeal of Colonial Virginia* (New York, 1975), was that slave owners thought black slaves as a class were important for maintaining social stability. Their color and differing physical characteristics made it relatively easy for the rich planters to use black slaves as a permanent underclass and thus claim racial equality existed for all whites irrespective of their origins or their economic status. In this manner planters would check any serious challenge to their dominance from socially and economically deprived subsistence farmers of the southern colonies, who constituted a majority of the population. Once the social and the economic benefits of slavery were recognized, the ruling classes of this seaboard region institutionalized the system.

Initially the southern colonies had been settled for investment and to produce cash crops for the mother country, England, according to the mercantilist theories of the seventeenth and eighteenth centuries. Unlike the New England and Middle Atlantic colonies, where self-sufficient farming and free white labor quickly developed as the norm, the southern colonies continued their original system of one-crop plantations or farms on which black slaves performed most of the manual labor. At the same time, poorer whites in the tidewater regions and yeoman farmers who were beginning to exploit the foothills of the Appalachian range (known also as the back-country) found themselves increasingly dependent on the trade and certainly the society of the tidewater planters. To a certain extent this relationship continued for nearly a century, inculcating a unique culture that was based economically on raising crops for profit and socially on black slavery.

In contrast, northern farm communities engaged in diversified farming for local markets. The surplus that accrued was not invested in more land and slaves, as in the extractive agricultural economy of the South, but in commerce, fisheries, and eventually in industrial growth. At first much of the surplus in the North was invested in capital improvements: land, buildings, fences, equipment, and the like. These investment practices gave rise to the hardy though misleading stereotypes of the "Industrious North" and the "Lazy South."

Certainly New England and the Middle Atlantic colonies possessed a different climate and geography as well as a different society from that of the rural South. With many variations, of course, the colonies north of Virginia and Maryland tended to evolve around the village and town community, which served both a market and a social need. Whereas a traveler in the plantation South could ride for miles without encountering any sign of human habitation, another traveler in New England or in the Middle Atlantic colonies on the other hand would notice the concentration of towns and villages. Population density in the North tended to be almost double that of comparative areas of the South as a result of (1) the market-oriented monoculture in the South where the greatest profits could be made from exploiting virgin land; and (2) the lack of suitable open range in the North for raising livestock because of colder winter climates. Thus climate and a scarcity of fertile virgin lands, particularly in the Northeast, determined very early the pattern of development. The Puritan interlude in New England also contributed mightily to town building, community solidarity, and individual enterprise, whether it be in farming or in commercial and manufacturing ventures.

Although all of the colonies prior to the American Revolution had slave populations, northern economies were not conducive to the kind of widescale, extractive farming that made a servile labor force profitable or socially desirable. By the late eighteenth century slavery had been abolished in several northern states, while in others it was well on the road to extinction at the very time that it was becoming firmly fixed in the southern states. While the Founding Fathers were writing the Constitution in Philadelphia, economic and cultural differences were already defining the two regions. Moreover, the vast distances (by eighteenth- and early nineteenth-century standards) that separated the northern states from the southern were inadequately served by a transportation system consisting mainly of slow coastal vessels and wretched, poorly maintained roads. Still there were extensive connections between the North and the South. The early commercial trade between the two sections soon became more diversified. Services of benefit to the South such as marketing, crop insurance, and commission brokerage could be found in the northern colonies and European urban centers.

The Constitutional Debate on Slavery

The War of Independence fostered nationalism and brought the two sections closer in a common patriotic heritage. In the war's aftermath came the ratification of the Constitution, which was likewise a unifying agent. But the debates at the Philadelphia Convention disclosed some troublesome differences between the two sections that were patched over but never settled. The institution of slavery was a fundamental problem for which the convention found only a temporary solution. The question of including slaves as part of a state's population for the purpose of determining representation in the House of Representatives and for the election of the president and vice president was an issue that elicited sharply divergent views. Northern delegates were generally opposed to any enumeration of slaves as a basis for any state's representation in the new government while many of the southern delegates demanded complete enumeration. The deadlock was finally broken by the compromise of counting each slave as three-fifths of a person.

A much more significant difference of opinion, however, concerned the slave trade. South Carolina, Georgia, and North Carolina maintained that any constitution that might be adopted should explicitly forbid the government from interfering with the international slave trade. At this time there was no regional distinctiveness to the debate. The Deep South, which was then beginning to exploit virgin lands to the west, lacked cheap labor and demanded that the trade remain unrestricted. New England delegates, influenced perhaps by their continuing economic interests in the profitable slave trade but also concerned about the fate of the Constitution, sided with their colleagues in the lower seaboard slave states in supporting a continuation of the trade. The opposition of Virginia and Maryland, which contested the trade on moral grounds, can be explained in part by the rapid decline of tobacco production in those states because of soil exhaustion, and hence a concomitant decline in the profitability of slavery. But antislavery attitudes that resulted from the natural rights ideology of the Revolution and the political ideas that Thomas Jefferson and other Virginia leaders fostered cannot be ignored either. Their collective judgments were voiced eloquently on the floor of the convention. George Mason, the rich Virginia planter, told his fellow delegates that slavery was both a moral evil and a national calamity. Nevertheless, a compromise was effected that permitted the slave trade to continue until 1808. A fugitive slave clause was also inserted at the insistence of delegates from the Deep South. In deference to the feelings and beliefs of a majority of the delegates, the words "slaves" or "slavery" did not appear in the completed document. Rather the word "persons" was substituted whenever mention was made of servitude. Ironically, this choice of words would become an important aspect of the antislavery argument that free soilers like Abraham Lincoln and Salmon P. Chase would advance fifty years later.

Luther Martin of Maryland, like Mason a delegate from a border slave state, summarized for his state's assembly the majority opinion of the convention on slavery. The national government under the proposed constitution, he said, should work towards "the gradual abolition of slavery and the emancipation of the slaves already in the states." The convention held that slavery was "inconsistent with the genius of republicanism, and has a tendency to destroy those principles on which it is supported, as it lessens the sense of the equal rights of mankind and habituates us to tyranny and oppression."
Charles Pinckney, a delegate from South Carolina, ob-

jected sharply to these noble sentiments. To him slaves were simply a form of cheap labor indispensable to the plantation economies of the Lower South. He said on the convention floor that if he "and all his colleagues were to sign the Constitution and use their personal influence, it would be of no avail towards obtaining the assent of their Constituents." He put his argument succinctly. "S. Carolina & Georgia cannot do without slaves," he said, "as to Virginia she will gain by stopping the importations. Her slaves will rise in value, & she has more than she wants." The ideology of the Revolution enjoyed almost as much currency in South Carolina as in Virginia. Planters of the Lower South accepted the Declaration of Independence but simply ignored the document's antislavery intimations. The difference between Virginia and South Carolina is best explained in part by subtle differences in political philosophy and also by the eighteenth-century decline of plantation monoculture in the Chesapeake region.

Regional Development and New Discord

Although it was not exclusively sectional interests that brought about the slave clauses in the Constitution, one must recognize that the ramifications of slavery very much affected the new nation. In states such as South Carolina slaves made up almost 50 percent of the total population. And only twelve years after the termination of slave importation in 1808 came the sectional clash over the admission of Missouri that called forth Thomas Jefferson's premonition of the "firebell in the night." The fugitive slave clause in the Constitution resulted in the Congressional Act of 1793 that empowered either a federal or state magistrate to judge the claims of a master in the retrieval of a fugitive. But as the popular view regarding slavery began to change during the early years of the nineteenth century, the question of returning fugitive slaves grew in importance. Many northern states passed personal liberty laws that sought to block the 1793 Act.

During that period attitudes of the Upper South towards

the peculiar institution began to change also, but more in defense of slavery than in opposition to it. The moral objections to slavery voiced earlier, combined with what was perceived to be the problem of racial tension in the Upper South, had led to the formation of a colonization movement, a program of emancipating and relocating blacks to Africa or to other areas of the world where they could then set up sovereign states. Virginia had led all other states in establishing colonization societies. By the 1820s the movement had gone into a rapid decline south of the Mason-Dixon line, however. The antislavery sentiment that existed in the country began to migrate north after the Missouri debates in 1820–1821.

At about the same time, cultural and economic differences that had always tended to separate the two regions took on new significance. The economic growth of the South was fast overriding moral qualms about slavery. Most of the tillable land in the lower seaboard slave states was suitable for the production of only short-staple cotton. But unlike long-staple cotton, which could be grown profitably only in very restricted areas of the South and which could be spun into high-quality cloth that could bear the labor-intensive costs of seed removal, short-staple cotton could furnish only poorer grades of cloth because of the difficulty of removing the seeds and spinning the fibers. This problem was partly overcome when Eli Whitney invented a cheap, mechanical method for seed removal with his cotton gin in 1793. At this time also British technology had just developed power-driven spinners and looms that could convert short-staple fibers into cloth. Short-staple cotton quickly became a prime commodity in such wide areas of the Deep South that it had a profound effect on the economies of all the slave states.

The industrial revolution that began in northern Europe, especially in Great Britain, during the last quarter of the eighteenth century had rapidly spread to New England and the Middle Atlantic states. Technological advances in motive power and in textile production together with a general increase in living standards after the conclusion of the Napoleonic Wars created an expanding market for all commodities but especially for cotton, which was unaffected by the Corn Laws in Britain that protected its home market from American foodstuffs. Cheap cotton cloth for the masses became widespread and generated an expanding cotton market and an ever-increasing demand for cheap labor, which in the American South meant slave labor. The cotton gin was one in a series of inventions (the only one outside of Great Britain) that contributed to the world's first fully mechanized industry. Manufacturers could now undersell handwoven cloth anywhere in the world, including India and China. This development reinforced the original "colonial" character of southern society.

The need for slave labor vastly exceeded the numbers available, and the supply was limited by the prohibition of slave importation. The slave population south of the Mason-Dixon line now shifted away from the border states, where cotton could not be grown profitably and where the fertility of plantation lands was now very nearly exhausted from a century of wasteful agricultural practices. Planters in those states soon found a profitable market for their surplus slaves in the Lower South, however. The immorality of slavery in the Atlantic border states became for many a quaint idea. Although domestic slave trading in the antebellum years was not considered an honorable vocation, and although slave breeding for the market in the cotton states was denied emphatically, both practices yielded high profits and were carried on extensively. Because of the dubious nature of these enterprises, few records were kept and fewer yet have come down to us. Frederic Bancroft, in his work *Slave Trading in the Old South* (2 vols., Baltimore, 1931), relates how difficult it was for him to uncover hard evidence of the domestic slave trade.

The cultural differences stemming from the early patterns of colonial settlement, character of immigration, and relative isolation of the sections from each other had become much more sharply defined as modernization brought changes to the values and the economies of the free states and as worldwide demand for cotton started a process of rationalizing and ex-

panding the cotton culture of the South. Economic development of the sections followed diverging paths. Westward expansion north of the Missouri Compromise line carried New
England attitudes and capital and enterprise into the Northwest, which had been proclaimed a free territory first by the
Northwest Ordinance of 1787 then later by the Missouri Compromise of 1820. At the same time the slave-plantation system
had extended its culture and its values westward south of the
Compromise line excepting the state of Missouri, the only
slave state north of that boundary.

Gideon Welles, northern newspaper editor and Democratic politician, gives us a graphic though one-sided account
of these cultural differences on the eve of the Mexican-American War. He visited a trade fair in Washington, D.C. during
the spring of 1846 and did not remember seeing among "the
very great variety of specimens of skill, ingenuity and industry
. . . a single article made south of the Potomac." The trade fair
coincided with racing week, which gave Welles an opportunity
to draw an invidious comparison between vacationing southerners at the race track ("They own the horses, they make the
bets") and the frugal, industrious northerners who "busily engaged . . . in examining everything to be seen, hearing everything to be heard, and have brought some specimens of their
handiwork to pay the expenses of their journey."

The application of steam power to the railroads, as it had
been earlier applied to the textile industry, had speeded up the
modernization process and revolutionized market potential in
Europe. Railroads had a similar though delayed impact in the
United States. By the mid-1830s railroad projects were vying
with canals and turnpikes for the scarce capital available. At
first the slave states were as receptive as the free states to the
benefits of railroad transportation. Indeed, the first railroad
venture in the nation was planned and executed in Maryland.
And South Carolina soon followed with a line from Charleston
to Hamburg, just north of the Savannah River port of Augusta,
Georgia. But investment in slaves and land ate up southern

capital and precluded any extensive railroad construction. Thereafter, until the 1850s, the pace of railroad development in the North far outstripped that in the South. Many of the cotton states could and did depend on the Mississippi River and its tributaries for transportation of their staples, but these and other river arteries were inflexible trade routes that left much of the South deprived of markets and connections with the outside world. Until the decade before the Civil War, when southern railroad expansion reached a takeoff point, most of the rural South was virtually isolated. Railroad, canal, and turnpike development, a concomitant for the emergence of any industrial state, tended first to emphasize the disparity in economic growth between the two regions, then to reinforce sectional identity. The telegraph too, which arrived in the 1840s, promoted regional loyalties before it contributed to and emphasized national unity.

Another medium of communication that technological advances stimulated was newspapers. The application of steam power to the new rotary presses helped to make the advent of metropolitan dailies possible. Newspapers were still comparatively expensive, but through semiweekly and weekly editions they reached a wide audience, especially in rural areas. And despite the high cost of rag newsprint, penny presses were established in New York and other cities which brought news and opinion to the poorer classes. Aspiring politicians quickly realized the power that editors and publishers could command in influencing the public. As early as the 1820s the press had become not just a political device but a powerful medium for persuasion on social issues. John M. Niles, a Jacksonian Democrat from Connecticut, himself a former newspaper editor, noted how the press, in this instance the southern press, was promoting sectionalism in the mid-1840s. "With a Southern President, and a Southern press, to direct and form public sentiment," said Niles, "is it to be wondered at that Southern influence has obtained an ascendancy greatly exceeding the real merit of the one or the intrinsic strength of the other?"

As controversy over slavery became more pronounced, much of the press of both regions indulged in irresponsible journalism. Some conservative Democratic and Whig newspapers sought to prevent sectional conflict and questioned the patriotism of those who raised divisive issues. But many more journals on each side of the Mason-Dixon line, seeking higher circulation, pictured the institutions of the other region in most unflattering terms that owed little to accuracy and much to sensational exaggeration. There is no doubt that after a quarter of a century of such constant editorial bashing, the southern and northern publics could believe the worst of each other. Professional politicians, of course, found it profitable for their careers to harp on the evils of the other section. And as the noted historian Roy F. Nichols has pointed out in his *Disruption of American Democracy* (New York, 1948), local control of the election machinery meant that campaigns for office featuring these themes in abusive rhetoric were being held everywhere in the Union at the rate of one a month.

Between the press and the politicians, cultural stereotypes became quite firmly fixed in the minds of the American public. Horace Bushnell, the well-traveled and sophisticated theologian, had this to say about the South in 1860. "I really pity, and from the bottom of my heart, those wretched slave-holding sections of the country. Between so many fears, so much pride and poverty and jealousy, so many wild tempers and so many appalling weaknesses, it must be just now, next thing to a hell upon earth to be their lot." William Howard Russell, the famous war correspondent for the London *Times* found just as much vehemence in southern hatred of the North. "Whether it be the consequence of some secret influence which slavery has upon the minds of men, or . . . aggression of the north upon their institutions," he observed, "the deepest animosity and most vindictive hate" has excited "something like ferocity in the southern mind towards New England, which exceeds belief." If one adds the agitation of a worldwide abolitionist movement to the volatile mixture, one could count on an eventual explosion, or as William H. Seward put it in a memorable speech, an "irrepressible conflict." Seward, a leading northern statesman, was speaking for an emerging industrial state in which free labor and entrepreneurial capitalism were finding it impossible to coexist with a slave-based agrarian economy and its associated values. He spoke also for the educated, middle classes of the North who found the institution of slavery a moral blot on the vaunted pretensions of a democratic republic. As these individuals hoped for a humane accommodation to the new technology, so they were increasingly insistent that the primitive barbarism of slavery not be tolerated in the new order of things.

Impact of Reform

Even before the Napoleonic Wars, there was evidence of other kinds of resistance to many of the abrupt social changes brought about by the emerging industrial state. Opposition to "the dark satanic mills" was particularly evident in Great Britain, where the machine age had begun earlier and where it was advancing more rapidly than elsewhere. Robert Owen, proprietor of cotton mills at New Lanark, near Glasgow, Scotland, was one of the many middle-class manufacturers in Britain who understood the social implications of modernization and sought to make reform of working conditions in the new factories a matter of public policy. Owen began his program in 1813. Others in Britain and on the Continent, notably Claude Saint-Simon, contributed to a widening demand for reform.

Significantly, it was the modernizing process itself which expanded in numbers and in influence the middle classes to which most of the reformers belonged. This release of human energy, this increase and distribution of wealth, created a surge of leisure time activity which, combined with an improvement in educational opportunities, focused more and more attention on social and economic injustice. Novelists like Charles Dickens dramatized graphically the miserable lot of the poor and the working classes to middle-class audiences in Great Britain and the United States. The popularity of his books in the

United States, where he traveled widely and lectured to thousands, helped make reform a middle-class initiative. The effects of urbanization, too, were brought to public attention. The evils of the metropolis were multiplied when the villages and towns of the seventeenth century were rapidly transformed into cities of the nineteenth century.

The reform movement was a protean force that embraced world peace, women's rights, temperance, prison and asylum reform, utopian schemes, public health, even special diets for rich and poor alike. But early on a movement of considerably older origin, the abolition of slavery, began to claim major attention. The consummate evils of the slave trade were the object of exposure and reform as early as the mid-eighteenth century. Quakers in Britain and in the American colonies were particularly earnest in their efforts to stamp out the trade. Already the revolutionary government in France had abolished slave trade and slavery itself in France and its colonies. William Wilberforce and Thomas Clarkson, British reformers and indefatigable opponents of slavery, were successful in their efforts to eliminate the external slave trade in Britain and British possessions in 1808, the same year that the Constitution terminated it in the United States. In 1833 they succeeded in having Parliament abolish slavery in all British colonies.

American reformers, like their British counterparts, espoused a broad spectrum of reforms, but unlike the British experience, slavery was not a far and distant thing to them; it was an integral part of the American Republic. Thus the abolition movement quickly claimed major attention and elicited a hostile reaction from the slave states and from moderates everywhere who were concerned about the fate of the Union.

For some time the slavery question had been muted by an unwritten political covenant between the two sections, but it remained a constant threat to the political parties that sought to bridge sectional difficulties. Since the reestablishment of the two-party system in 1828, first the Democrats and then the Whigs managed to create an intersectional party structure that tended to separate the elements that tended to separate the sections and their diverging cultures. A growing professionalization of politics (or "the partisan imperative" as one historian has called it) had kept a national two-party system in existence. But the question of slavery continued to intrude. During the mid-1830s ex-President John Quincy Adams, then a congressman from Massachusetts, publicized the issue with his dramatic fight for the right to present antislavery petitions. The furious reaction of slave state congressmen to his and other abolitionist tactics furnished vivid material to the press of the North and South for an extended period of time.

The evolution of the antislavery protest into the more moderate and constitutionally acceptable free-soil position contributed mightily to the debate. For the first time southerners were confronted with the prospect of the eventual elimination of slavery, and with it a complete readjustment of their way of life. World public opinion was now condemning the practice of slavery. And southerners were beginning to harbor suspicions that many of their own countrymen in the North were joining in what had the appearance of a crusade against slavery. A siege mentality was overtaking the South.

The conclusion of the Mexican-American War nearly ignited a blast that sundered the Union. National attention had been drawn to the disposition of the Mexican cession. Should this territory become slave or free or part slave, part free? Politicians managed to defuse the crisis in the Compromise of 1850. But the combustible materials, those deeply ingrained sectional prejudices, were still smouldering. As the debate over the future of the Union became more strident during the 1850s a kind of mass paranoia developed, with each section fearing the intentions of the other. The national organization of the Whig party began to collapse under internal pressures after 1852. Even before these events Protestant churches, which had been an intercultural link, were dividing into northern and southern wings. For a brief period nativistic movements sought to fill the political vacuum by drawing attention to the alleged undesirable characteristics of new immigrants. But even their political organization, the American party, soon separated into geographic factions that were termed the "North American" and the "South American" organizations.

Free Soilers, North Americans, and northern Whigs finally coalesced as the Republican party and went into the presidential campaign of 1856 on a purely sectional platform that openly opposed the extension of slavery. For those politicians who were sensitive to the problems besetting the Union, the appearance of the Republican party was a dangerous thing. Former president Martin Van Buren, veteran of many a campaign, declared that though slavery had had some effect on all the political contests of the past, never until the emergence of the Republican party had it posed such a challenge to the Union. "[This is] the first time in our history," he said, "one side and that the one in which we reside has undertaken to carry an election including the control of the Federal Government, and against the united wishes of the other." To Van Buren the two-party balance had been destroyed. He was almost as despairing as Calhoun had been six years before about the continued existence of the Union.

And so the slow-growing virus of slavery that had infected the colonies in 1619 was finally incapacitating the Union. Many remedies had been employed to halt its progress, but they had been unavailing. In 1860 the triumph of the Republican party in the presidential election spelled the end of the old Union and made a war between the sections virtually certain. Henry Adams had thought the Union more a sentiment than a reality. Jefferson Davis, new President of the Confederate States, would have agreed with him, but not Abraham Lincoln and a host of northerners who regarded the Union as an indissoluble compact that could not be abrogated. The vast potential for economic development, as they saw it for themselves and for future generations, must not be impaired. "Many independent men everywhere in these States," said Lincoln in his first annual address to Congress on December 3, 1861, "a few years back in their lives, were hired laborers. The prudent, penniless beginner in the world, labors for wages awhile, saves a surplus with which to buy tools or land for himself; then labors on his own account another while, and at length hires another new beginner to help him. This is the just, and generous, and prosperous system, which opens the way to all—gives hope to all, and consequent energy, and progress, and improvement of condition to all."

By this time, Seward's irrepressible conflict had come to pass. Four years of bitter, bloody civil war would determine that the future lay with an integrated democratic republic where free labor and expansive capitalism were the dominant forces. The best efforts of temporizing politicians who had worked over the past forty years to accommodate the opposites of slavery and freedom within one organic state had failed as many had foretold. The guns that bombarded Fort Sumter on a stormy dawn in April 1861 abruptly and violently smashed in a few hours the old federal Union and the paradox of freedom coexisting with slavery in a modernizing nation state.

CHAPTER ONE

Tensions

On March 4, 1837, a short, balding man flanked by two tall, thin men stepped forward on the east portico of the Capitol in Washington. The short, balding man was Martin Van Buren, and he had just taken the oath of office as eight President of the United States. Chief Justice Roger B. Taney, one of the tall, thin men, had administered the oath to Van Buren. The other tall, thin man remained with Taney in the background. But he scarcely went unnoticed by the dense crowd that had formed beneath the portico. He was Andrew Jackson, who in effect had chosen Van Buren to be his successor.

Van Buren began to speak in a rapid, rather high-pitched voice that did not carry to the outer reaches of the crowd. His address radiated confidence in the state of the nation. Yet he said, "I must go into the Presidential chair the inflexible and uncompromising opponent of every attempt on the part of Congress to abolish slavery in the District of Columbia against the wishes of the slaveholding States, and also with a determination equally decided to resist the slightest interference with it in the states where it exists." That he, the most experienced and skillful politician in the country, indeed the principal creator of the modern Democratic party, should have been so explicit about slavery betrays his concern about the dangers it posed to the stability of the Union. Like other perceptive statesmen of his generation, he was sensitive to the differences that existed between the sections of his enormous, loosely knit country. And he was well aware of the divisive forces that these differences bred and how they expressed themselves in challenges to the legal and constitutional framework of the country.

Although he seemed confident about the prosperous condition of the national economy, privately Van Buren was worried about the tempo of speculation in western lands, in eastern city lots, in commodities and in securities, especially railroad and canal bonds. As Vice President and the intimate advisor of President Jackson, he had approved the issuance of the "Specie Circular" that directed the government land office to accept only gold and silver or the notes of specie-paying banks for payment on the public lands. He was concerned about the solvency of the nation's overextended state-chartered banks—those that were neither participants in state reinsurance systems nor operating under the Deposit Banking Act of the previous year. These economic worries were compounded by the appearance of a concerted antislavery campaign.

Abolitionism and National Politics

Not long after Van Buren's comments on slavery in his inaugural address, William Slade, a congressman from Vermont with abolitionist leanings, opened up the debate anew in the second session of the Twenty-fifth Congress with a scathing attack on the institution of slavery before he was gagged at the insistence of southern colleagues. Former President John Quincy Adams, now a congressman from Massachusetts, had dramatized the right of petition when he first presented abolitionist petitions in 1836. These petitions were a new tactic of the abolitionists and were usually couched in language that avoided outright demands for abolition but that still stigmatized slavery and also referred in caustic terms to the slave owners themselves. The furious reaction of southern slave owners, headed by John C. Calhoun of South Carolina in the Senate and by Henry A. Wise of Virginia in the House, was as disturbing to Van Buren as the steady persistence of Gerrit Smith of New York and Samuel May of Massachusetts, principal organizers of the abolition campaign, as well as the vitriolic editorials in William Lloyd Garrison's *Liberator*, the most controversial of the abolitionist newspapers.

Prior to this time Van Buren and his allies in Congress had successfully imposed a House rule that automatically tabled abolition petitions before they could be read. The Senate followed suit. But Adams through various parliamentary loopholes had kept the issue before Congress and the public. Dubbed by his admirers as "Old Man Eloquent," he infuriated his slaveholding colleagues when he subjected them in his shrill voice to merciless criticism for their denial of an ancient Anglo-American right that he maintained was one of the basic principles of representative democracy and which was specifically protected by the First Amendment to the Constitution. Threatened with censure and even expulsion from the House, Adams persisted in his course. Each session he gained additional votes for repeal of the rule. Finally in 1844, by a vote of 108 to 80, the gag rule was lifted. But the controversy demonstrated the widening rift between the two sections as well as the latent antislavery bias of the northern states, and perhaps also their growing strength and self-consciousness.

Obviously it was the educated and the articulate in the free and the slave states that publicized the congressional debate on the right of petition during the early years of the Van Buren administration. Antislavery societies were being established throughout the northern states but were disappearing from the greater Chesapeake region. A dozen or more newspapers were now devoting their editorial pages to abolition. While condemning unsparingly slavery everywhere as cruel, inhuman, and immoral servitude, they were concentrating their attack on the institution in areas where they felt Congress clearly had the power to abolish it: the District of Columbia, the territories, and the domestic slave trade.

But the growing disparity in population, in wealth, and in other material resources between the free and the slave regions as well as an increasing distinctiveness in culture to which slavery was a significant contributing factor were also important reasons for eventual separation and war. Abolitionist leaders as well as southern defenders of slavery followed the census returns that showed that the population of the free states had increased from 6.8 million in 1830 to 9.5 million in 1840. Population in the South, which was about 60 percent of that of the North in 1830, had declined to about half that of the North in 1840.

The House of Representatives, whose membership was based on the census returns for each state, reflected this growing disparity. Even counting three-fifths of the slave population (as the federal Constitution provided), free states increased their majority from twenty-three seats in 1830 to twenty-nine seats by 1840. The disparity expressed in total seats was 149 representatives from the free states to 88 from the slave states. Later the South would gain one seat from the territory of Florida, but the North would gain at least three seats when the territories of Michigan, Iowa, and Wisconsin became states. And a portent of a grim future for the South was the flood of white immigrants that was pouring into northern cities, farms, and workshops. The fact that most of these immigrants came from western Europe, particularly Great Britain and the German states, where public opinion strongly opposed slavery, further polarized attitudes and reinforced a growing sectional animosity. And an important development in the political system was the integration of these immigrant voters into the political power structure. Specific events punctuated these long-term trends.

In the closing months of the Jackson administration, the huge southwestern territory of Texas gained its independence from Mexico. Peopled largely by southerners, the new Republic of Texas accepted slavery and under the leadership of Sam Houston began efforts to become a state in the Union. The Jackson administration recognized the independence of Texas, but deferred any further action. Van Buren made no mention of Texas in his inaugural address. Recognizing the political danger in adding to the Union what could be several slave states in the southwest, he effectively quashed any annexation move for the next four years. But he and other moderate political figures recognized that the Texas issue would eventually surface again with disruptive force.

And it did. After Van Buren's term two southern leaders who at the time were outside of mainstream partisan politics, John C. Calhoun and President John Tyler, sought to capitalize on the Texas issue. In doing so, they briefly captured the public mood, and despite the best efforts of the two main party leaders, Henry Clay and Martin Van Buren, to sidetrack Texas annexation, it became the compelling issue in the presidential election of 1844. On March 1, 1845, President Tyler signed into law the bill admitting Texas to statehood.

Emerging Sectionalism

Once annexation was an accomplished fact, sectional politics again assumed major importance. Supporters and opponents of further annexation, who saw in it an enormous expansion of slave territory, intensified their agitation. The Democratic party bowed to southern urgings and also what was deemed broad popular support in backing a policy of westward expansion even if it brought on a war with Mexico. Whig leaders, though more moderate in espousing westward expansion, also accepted the slogan of "manifest destiny." There were signs in both parties however, that Whigs and Democrats in the free states were questioning expansion if it meant creating more slave territory.

Abolitionist groups, which had first found political expression in the Liberty party that participated in the election of

1840, now became a cause for increasing concern to the intersectional party structure. The reaction of such moderate party leaders as Henry Clay was a manifestation of the uneasiness felt toward what they perceived to be a divisive development that imperilled the Union. A shaky two-party system had come into being during the decade between 1830 and 1840. The Jacksonians, a spin-off from the Jeffersonian Republican party, dominated party politics and controlled the federal government. Professing states' rights, wise and frugal government, and equality of opportunity in the Jeffersonian tradition, the principles of the new Democratic party were shot through with paradoxes. Extolling republican virtue, an idealistic but vague view of human nature and political behavior drawn from a previous age, the Jacksonians professed impartial leadership. But at the same time they considered the acquisition of political office or "spoils" to be the foundation of a government administered by partisans from the President down to the lowest tidewaiter or postal clerk. The Jacksonian slogan "equal rights" more often than not was observed in the breach. Equality of opportunity was not applied to the Indians, the free blacks, the slaves, the thousands of poor farmers north and south who found the best western lands being rapidly engrossed by speculators or priced off the mass market by restrictive land policies, nor was it applied to the factory workers and most immigrants in the new cities and mill towns. These submerged groups were not participants in a social contract, which placed a premium on individual enterprise rather than communal or state responsibility for the welfare and advancement of the people as a whole. Jacksonian orators and presses claimed that there had been a restoration of eighteenth-century values, while party leaders kept their eyes on the alluring opportunities offered by an industrializing society in the North and an expanding, slave-plantation system in the South.

The vast influx of immigrants of the late 1840s and early 1850s, most of whom crowded into urban centers that were ill-prepared for their reception, made large areas of cities like New York, Boston, and Philadelphia filthy, disease- and

crime-ridden slums. Public policy was anything but equalitar-
ian for underprivileged members of society. But its optimistic
vision of American society did provide energy and momentum
and even public support for certain vigorous entrepreneurial
elements. There was still opportunity to be grasped in the fluid
society of antebellum America. The ambitious, hard-working
white male, whether a native American or a recent immigrant,
whether from a factory family or from a subsistence farm,
could improve his material lot far more rapidly than in the
static, class-structured social order of the old world. Despite
its internal contradictions the emphasis the Democratic party
placed on individual enterprise gave this aspect of human
endeavor a certain permanence in the popular attitudes of
the day.

One can notice this ethic operating in the career of Horace
Greeley, who became the most influential newspaper editor of
the antebellum years. As a penniless, self-taught printer's ap-
prentice who had been brought up on a Vermont farm, Greeley
drifted to New York City in 1831. He found typesetting jobs
scarce in the metropolis. He was down to his last dollar when
he managed to secure a typesetting position simply because
no other printer in the city would take it. The job was the
composition of a tiny New Testament whose layout consisted
of double columns of agate type with a text that had many
notes in Greek and italics throughout to emphasize passages.
Never a rapid typesetter, Greeley prided himself on his accuracy. As he explained "my proofs on this work at first looked
as though they had caught the chicken pox." Greeley labored
on this job from twelve to fourteen hours a day for a wage
that varied between five and six dollars a week, which barely
paid for his room and board. Ten years later Greeley founded
the *New York Tribune*, which became the oracle of the free
states and even maintained a respectable circulation south of
the Mason-Dixon line.

There were thousands of would-be Horace Greeleys in the
nation, though few would reach the eminence in their various
professions of that great journalist. They had all been willing,

even eager to brave hardship, and even hunger on occasion and were always ready to accept desperately hard work for long hours under frequently miserable conditions of employment for what they hoped would be material advancement. Alexis de Tocqueville noticed this almost universal passion for work and commented favorably upon it.

While in general agreement with Tocqueville, Michel Chevalier, the French Saint-Simonian who visited the United States at about the same time, made a shrewd observation on how the work ethic was promoting sectional trends in Jacksonian America. Chevalier saw an emerging conflict between the commercial-industrializing North that was based on a free labor economy and the plantation South's slave labor economy. As these differing features of socioeconomic development were becoming visible, he observed their impact on the political evolution of the nation. "The principle of separation," he said, "is engaged in a deadly conflict with the spirit of centralization or consolidation." The work ethic so prized by the French bourgeoisie during the early years of Louis Philippe's reign colored Chevalier's narrative. As a result he tended to distort the extent of Yankee influence. He regarded the New Englander as the colonizer of the nation, "the arbiter of manners and customs." "It is from him that the country has taken a general hue of austere severity, that is religious and even bigoted. . . . It is he that has introduced the Prison Reform, multiplied schools, founded temperance societies." But the incongruity of slavery in a republic that extolled human rights offended the French visitor. During his travels through the South, he concluded that the blacks were "treated as if they did not belong to the human race." "Free or slave," he wrote in a harsh vein, "the black is here denied all that can give him the dignity of man. The law forbids the instruction of the slave or the free man of colour in the simplest rudiments of learning, under the severest penalties; the slave has no family; he has no civil rights; he holds no property."

Nor did the lot of the average white worker in the industrialized North comport with Jacksonian optimism. In 1838 more than one-third of the workers in New York City were unemployed. Some ten thousand persons, said the *New Yorker* on January 20, 1838, were "in utter and hopeless distress with no means of surviving the winter but that provided by charity." These comments were made in the midst of a deep depression. But George Henry Evans, the British-born agrarian reformer, wrote in 1844 that "thirty years ago the number of paupers in the whole United States was estimated at 29,166, or one in three hundred. The pauperism of New York City now amounts to 51,600 or one in every seven of the population." Even skilled workers, always in short supply, witnessed a decline in real wages between 1837 and 1858. At the same time the cost of living increased about 20 percent. Skilled workers found it increasingly difficult to maintain a decent living standard during this period, and the income of the semiskilled and the unskilled was well below the poverty line. Yet Jacksonian rhetoric and the astute management of its political organization, where workingmen leaders through control of local offices eased the worst hardships of their less fortunate associates, allowed the party to pose with considerable success as the friend of labor. On a national scale, the Jacksonians, again relying on organization and avoidance of sectional issues, were able to form a national consensus in the government of a nation with so many conflicting interests.

States' Rights: Theory and Practice

Still, from its formation in 1828, this uneasy coalition of slave-owning planters and northern entrepreneurs clashed frequently over the direction of public policy. The tariff policy that party leadership framed subjected the new Democratic organization to intense strains between the free-trading South and the high-tariff demands of the emergent manufacturing interest of the North, culminating with the protective tariff of 1828. South Carolina political leader and Vice President of the United States John C. Calhoun, disappointed in his political ambitions and fearful for the future of the plantation South, challenged the protective tariff policy. He believed it to be simply a pretext for creating a national state on the Hamiltonian model based on free white labor at the expense of the slave-plantation system. Calhoun mounted an attack on the so-called "Tariff of Abominations" that was based on a strict interpretation of the Constitution. His definition of states' rights went far beyond the Jeffersonian ideas on limiting the powers of the central government that were expressed in the Virginia and Kentucky Resolutions of 1798. Calhoun followed convention when he insisted that sovereignty in its ultimate sense was indivisible but broke with the theories of John Marshall by assigning a preponderance of power to the states. To Calhoun the Union that was formed in 1789 was strictly a contractual arrangement that existed for the mutual benefit of all the states. Thus the central government that was established continued in force within closely defined limits delegated to it, and only while it adhered to the strict letter of the contract as defined by the states. Any state could and should nullify a federal law that it believed broke the original contract, especially if the legislation dealt inequitably with the social and economic well-being of a state or a region. Calhoun gave real expression to the position Jefferson had only intimated in the Kentucky Resolution of 1798.

The tariff of 1828 was a case in point. But beyond that dispute Calhoun's theory of nullification (or "interposition," as he preferred to call it) was an elaborate legal and institutional defense of the slave-plantation system. That socioeconomic order was being forced into a minority position as the industrial revolution, with its emphasis on free labor and private enterprise, gained momentum in the North. Calhoun was right in his economic assumptions over the long run. Southern cotton produced by slave labor helped mightily in creating a trade balance in favor of the North and a surplus in foreign exchange. These surpluses provided much of the capital that British and other foreign investors utilized to finance northern industrial growth.

The Compromise Tariff of 1833, which Calhoun and

Henry Clay arranged to patch over the differences between the sections on economic policy, was a stopgap measure and recognized as such by the principals involved. For a brief period, the constitutional and economic aspects of federal tariff policy ceased to be the focus of public debate. Four years later, public attention was drawn to the efforts of the new Van Buren administration to cope with the severe panic and ensuing Depression of 1837. The new administration had been in power for a scant thirteen days when financial panic erupted in the New York money market. The orgy of speculation in western lands, in city building lots, and in commodities, and overinvestment by the states and by private companies in canals and railroads, had come to an abrupt end. The panic swiftly spread to the commodity exchanges and the banks throughout the nation. Philip Hone, the New York businessman and diarist, described the panic's affect on the once-bustling city of New York. "No goods are selling, no business stirring, no boxes encumber the sidewalks of Pearl Street; stocks have fallen again . . . no remittances come from other states. . . . gold and silver, we have none, and there is no change either in our prospects or our currency." Over the next six years, the bank note circulation that had increased by 86 percent between 1834 and 1837 decreased about 59 percent by 1843.

On April 1, 1837, the deposit banks that held the nation's hard money reserves suspended specie payment. These suspensions and failures presaged a deep and lengthy depression that dampened entrepreneurial activity in the North and West and forced down commodity prices, especially for southern cotton. The depression, which quickly became worldwide, curtailed sharply European consumption of cotton, which in turn led planters to increase output in a vain attempt to recoup losses. Between 1831 and 1840, planters more than doubled the amount of cotton for export yet received one million dollars less for the export crop than they had the previous ten years. Until 1845 the hitherto expansive cotton economy of the South remained at a low ebb, promoting political discontent over real and fancied grievances with the policies of the national government.

But at first, the measures proposed by the Van Buren administration to deal with the depression gained the support of Calhoun and his southern states' rights contingent. They were especially attracted to the independent subtreasury system which Van Buren proposed. This measure would remove completely federal support from the banks and hence for private credit. To Calhoun's far-reaching mind this meant a curtailment of government support for the credit-hungry manufacturing interest that he was certain threatened the agrarian South. He and his followers believed that the proposed legislation would weaken significantly what they regarded as a centralizing trend and would be a consequent embarrassment to local sources of credit. Calhoun hoped that the drain on the southern economy by northern banks for credit and other services in marketing the cotton crop would be cut back if not halted completely. The result would be a strengthening of local financial resources in the South. None of these expectations was ever realized, though the subtreasury law was finally put into place in June 1840. It would be repealed by the Whig-dominated Twenty-seventh Congress in 1841 only to be reenacted when the Democrats returned to power in 1845. Specie reserves of the central government, the primary assets of the nation, would be separated from all private financial institutions until the passage of the National Banking Act during the Civil War.

Depression and the Second American Party System

The policy measures the Van Buren administration took to relieve the hardships of the depression had little or no impact on the workingmen in the cities of the nation, unemployed seamen, or small farmers everywhere, who were accustomed to earning money beyond their bare subsistence from marketing their surplus and in many instances from producing cloth in their homes under a putting-out system. (Often local merchants would furnish wool which was then woven into cloth in the home. The worker would deliver the finished product after receiving an agreed-upon sum for his labor.) In urban areas and factory towns throughout the Northeast, many manufacturers took advantage of the vast unemployment to break down the emerging trades union movement. And their efforts were in the main quite successful. Trade-union expansion came to an abrupt halt until economic prospects grew brighter in the late 1840s. Farmers too, along with planters large and small in the South, suffered though their economic situation was far better than that of the city workers.

While the Van Buren administration was seeking to rescue the public credit from the onslaught of the depression and dampening what it regarded as the divisive aspects of the antislavery movement, a new political coalition had come into being. There had always been opposition to the policies of the Jacksonians. It was not until the campaign and election of 1836, however, that a party platform expressing a specific program evolved and took on national dimensions. But the coalition that became the Whig party did not hold a national convention until 1840.

Some years earlier, opponents of Van Buren in New York state had capitalized on a sudden upsurge of public feeling against the Masonic order. A former Mason, William Morgan, had published a tract that claimed to reveal the secrets of the society. Soon thereafter, Morgan disappeared under mysterious circumstances that aroused the suspicions of transplanted Yankee farmers in western New York. Although his body was never recovered, the anti-Masonic movement quickly became a political protest. Enterprising politicians opposed to Van Buren's organization, the Albany Regency, seized upon the movement and after allying it with the National Republican opposition to the Jacksonians, created an effective political party. The anti-Masonic party spread to neighboring states in New England to the north and to Virginia and Maryland in the South. In 1831 the party held the nation's first nominating convention in Baltimore where it named for its presidential candidate William Wirt, famed lawyer, novelist, and attorney general in the Adams and Monroe administrations.

For the next five years, efforts were made to fuse the anti-Masons with the National Republicans and their successors, the Whigs. These attempts were eventually successful. The anti-Masons held their last convention as a separate party at Harrisburg, Pennsylvania, in 1836 where they nominated William Henry Harrison of Ohio for the presidency. Other candidates, Daniel Webster, Hugh Lawson White, formerly a Jacksonian, and Henry Clay, were all named by state conventions or legislative caucuses.

By 1840 the Whigs had perfected an organization largely through the efforts of Thurlow Weed, another New York politician as capable in his own way as Van Buren. In the spring of 1839, Weed journeyed to Washington, hopeful of persuading Daniel Webster to become the vice presidential nominee on a Harrison ticket. Webster opened the conversation by stating boldly that he would be the Whig candidate. Weed expressed his doubts. "Who then will be?" asked Webster. "It looks to me like Harrison," Weed replied. "Harrison has no chance," said Webster, "you are misinformed. The party will choose a man with longer civic experience, who is better adapted to the place." "The question is," said Weed, "who will poll the most votes?" "Well, very well, but what does that mean? You are going to choose a Scott delegation in New York." Weed explained that the reason for backing the popular veteran of the War of 1812, General Winfield Scott, was a move to weaken the Clay candidacy in the Empire State. He then sounded Webster on the vice presidency only to meet an instant and thunderous rebuff. Had Webster accepted, he would have been nominated at Harrisburg and would have become President upon Harrison's death, which was but a month after his inauguration. The fate of the Whig party would have certainly been different, and unquestionably the future of the nation would have taken a different course.

All of the candidates except White subscribed generally

to a program based on Hamiltonian ideas, as Henry Clay articulated them in his "American System." The new Whig party emphasized the role of the national government in planning the future of the nation. Frankly dedicated to stimulating manufacturing interests in the Northeast, Clay's program also appealed to the large established planters of the South because of its insistence on federally funded public works, canals and turnpikes at first, later railroads. The Whig party would bind northern manufacturers, whose mills consumed cotton, to the planter-producers of the staple. Improved means of transportation would inure to the benefit of both interests. A protective tariff and a national bank to provide easy credit would complement the national system of internal improvements and provide an expanding market for both raw and finished goods.

On the political side, the Whigs sought to capitalize on latent fears of executive tyranny by dedicating themselves to legislative supremacy. Although the Whig persuasion was not sharply defined and in many respects its rhetoric resembled that of the Jacksonians, it was sufficiently clear to attract the monied elites in all sections, particularly those who saw their future inhibited by the hard-money, free-trade policies of the Democrats. Whigs also, at least those in the free states, like the Manchester liberals in Britain, tended to be more receptive than the Democrats to moral causes. Hence antislavery sentiment was somewhat more attractive to them and to their leaders. This dangerous issue was a standing temptation for some northern Whig politicians to exploit because the chief opponents of their economic program happened also to be Democrats and slaveholders. But most Whig leaders were pragmatic enough to take a stand on slavery that was similar to that of the Democrats.

Politicians of both parties in the free states sought to reassure the slave states that public opinion in their section disavowed abolitionism, indeed regarded it as subversive and unlawful. Nor did the public image that abolitionists projected help the antislavery cause in the North. Like any reform movement during a period of economic and social stress, abolitionism attracted to it an assortment of unconventional, often-times fanatical types. Henry B. Stanton, husband of the feminist reformer Elizabeth Cady Stanton, has drawn a picture of such individuals. At an abolitionist convention in Boston, he observed "Father Lampson, so called, a crazy loon—his hair and flowing beard as white as driven snow . . . dressed in pure white, from head to foot, even including his shoes. . . . Abigail Folsom, another lunatic with a shock of unkempt hair reaching down to her waist. . . . George W. Mellon, clad in the military costume of the American Revolution and fancying himself to be General Washington. . . . Charles C. Burleigh . . . dressed like a tramp." But among these quirky individuals were leading figures of Boston society, all dedicated to the abolition of slavery—Wendell Phillips, the Brahmin of Boston Brahmins, Edmund Quincy, son of the president of Harvard, William Ellery Channing, the great Unitarian minister, the poet John Greenleaf Whittier, and of course William Lloyd Garrison, editor of the *Liberator*, the nation's leading aboli-tionist newspaper. To inspire this unusual group of the staid and the bizarre, the renowned gospel singers, the Hutchinson family, regaled all with the continuous recital of familiar hymns and antislavery songs until the speeches began.

However much the lunatic fringe may have given aboli-tionism a bad name, the antislavery movement certainly at-tracted the attention of politicians in the North. Governor William H. Seward of New York involved himself during 1839 and 1840 in controversies with Virginia, South Carolina, and Georgia over the return of fugitive slaves to bondage and the extradition for trial in southern courts of those who abetted the escape of slaves. In all instances Seward rejected the de-mands of southern governors, and asserted that none of the individuals they named for extradition had committed what was recognized as a crime in New York. He also declared that freedom, not slavery, was the natural condition of mankind. Abolitionists applauded Seward's stand, though it is fair to say that even conservative opinion in the North would have sup-ported Seward's contention. Southern opinion, expressed in the press, was outraged at such remarks and actions by a leading Whig politician and the chief executive of the richest, most populous state in the North.

Seward of course had been very careful to distance himself from the abolitionists, who were disparaged by the two major parties as either a tiny, irrational group of zealots or as troublemakers seeking to supplant white labor with black. Demagogic appeals in the North tended to inflame mobs that responded by sacking abolitionist presses and breaking up abolitionist meetings. Despite the assurances of conservative politicians both Whig and Democratic that the northern public would never tolerate any interference with slavery where it was lawfully established, more and more southern politicians, planters, and journalists came to view such professions with distrust.

Southern Fears

Mob actions against abolitionists in northern cities were expressions of mounting social and economic tensions stemming from the industrial revolution's restructuring of society. Similarly the furious defense of slavery from molders of southern opinion was as much a fear of internal tensions within southern society as it was alarm at external threats. For if there was a growing disparity in the distribution of wealth in the North, the situation in the South was much more inequitable. In a region where ownership of slaves conferred status and wealth, less than 10 percent of the white population held slaves. And of this 10 percent only a tiny fraction could be considered large planters, i.e., those who held from fifty to five hundred slaves. Still about one-third of white southerners belonged to slaveholding families.

By 1840, despite low cotton prices, the amount of capital required to become even a medium-sized planter was largely beyond the reach of most white southerners. Families of wealth and standing could never be sure about the stability of a social order that rested on slavery and that denied in large measure equality of opportunity. The isolation of the rural South from the mainstream of world opinion on slavery and the comparative lack of educational opportunity in the South made the southern masses susceptible to xenophobic encouragement.

Nor were northerners entirely free from exaggerated suspicions of southern culture. As railroads and later telegraph lines began to separate the North and the South into composite units, these improved means of transportation and communication tended to foster regional identity before they promoted national unity. These developments estranged the northern culture from the southern culture. As early as 1840 each section began to view the other as foreign soil. And though both sections shared a heritage, a language, and other social institutions, they would become in a short space of time alien from each other.

Calhoun, the most articulate and controversial spokesman for the slave states, increasingly referred to the South as the weaker section, reinforcing the underlying insecurity of the slave-plantation owners. And members of Congress who met for their sessions in the small, isolated southern city of Washington were forced to live close together in an environment that exaggerated sectional differences. The lifestyles of southern congressmen, many of whom came from rich plantation families, belied Calhoun's gloomy description of their section. James Henry Hammond, for instance, when a senator from South Carolina in the 1850s, spent large sums on lavish entertainment. The very capable manager of a highly productive plantation worked by four hundred slaves, Hammond gave an impression, albeit a false one, of the great wealth and strength of southern society. Hammond was not alone in this social display. The Falstaffian Howell Cobb of Georgia and the lean, erect James Chesnut, Jr., of South Carolina and his wife, the diarist Mary Boykin Chesnut, gave an aura of brilliance to Washington society during the Buchanan administration. Mrs. Roger Pryor, wife of the Virginia congressman and journalist, thought nothing of spending a small fortune for Worth gowns made from patterns imported from France and expertly fashioned to her figure. But the Washington scene was atypical of the country at large.

Calhoun and other southern leaders were well aware of the differing rates of economic growth between the two sections. Though the South was not deficient in entrepreneurial spirit, it had a chronic shortage of capital for investment in its railroad network and other means of transportation when compared to the resources that the North was deploying in these areas. By 1860, four northern states, New York, Pennsylvania, Illinois, and Ohio, had more railroad mileage than all of the fifteen slave states combined.

Perhaps more disturbing to the southern mind was the attitude of the entire Western world on slavery. Virtually all of western Europe was vehemently opposed to the institution. The Anti-Slavery Convention that met in London during June 1840 was an impressive demonstration of international pressure for abolition. The convention, arranged by the veteran English reformer Thomas Clarkson, featured a glittering list of European notables that included Queen Victoria's uncle, the Duke of Sussex, former Lord Chancellor Henry Brougham, Daniel O'Connell, the Irish leader, and François Guizot, the great historian and politician, who was then French minister to Great Britain. Among American representatives was James G. Birney of Cincinnati who later that year would be the presidential nominee of the Liberty party, the first American party to be organized on an antislavery basis.

Slavery was an issue, though a minor one, in the presidential campaign of 1840. The Whig nominee, William Henry Harrison, Virginia-born resident of Ohio and hero of the War of 1812, said nothing during the campaign on the slavery issue or on any other aspect of public policy. His opponent, Van Buren, was equally reticent. The Whigs waged a colorful campaign that was distinguished by theatrics like log cabins, hard cider, and coonskin caps, but little else except opposition to Van Buren, who was held responsible for hard times. Harrison won a resounding victory in the electoral college of 234 votes to 60 for Van Buren. The popular vote was much closer, however. Harrison's majority was only 146,315 votes out of 2,403,719 cast. Birney, the Liberty party candidate, polled about 7,000 votes. But veteran politicians in both major parties knew that these numbers did not reflect true antislavery strength. Determined defenders of slavery like Calhoun also looked beyond the election returns. They sensed the beginnings of a concerted movement to isolate and contain slavery where it existed as a preliminary move to abolishing the institution everywhere in the republic.

The High Tide of Reform

Calhoun was right. Abolition of slavery had become a distinct goal of a widespread reform movement that was beginning to proliferate throughout the Western world. The process of urbanization, a consequence of the industrial revolution, was creating a middle class which emphasized self-improvement, whether this be material success or educating one's self about the social and political issues of the times. The accumulation of wealth was providing more leisure time for newly educated and articulate groups, many of whom joined the ranks of the abolitionists.

Middle-class women were liberated from the hard work of the small, self-contained farms that characterized the Northeast in the early nineteenth century. With more leisure time they were able to devote themselves to rearing children or to furthering moral causes. What modern historians have referred to as "the cult of domesticity" was in reality a division of labor and responsibility on a gender basis. Middle-class men were expected to provide the means for maintaining comfortable homes. But the home itself became the woman's province. Women were considered to be naturally equipped to provide the aesthetic and moral qualities of the home. Men were the providers; they went out into the coarse, hard-driving arena of business, the professions, or politics or engaged in an arduous, possibly even life-threatening career in the military. Notable exceptions to this social order were the ministers, mainly Protestant, who preached the old Puritan verities that now included the notion of Christian stewardship and the responsibility of the wealthy to improve society. Moral uplift was the core of their message, and influential revivalists such as Charles Grandison Finney popularized this theme and created a special bond between ministers and middle-class women.

The revivals that swept middle-class America during the 1840s and 1850s helped create an emotional climate, especially in the free states, that contributed to antislavery sentiment. Middle-class clergymen like Henry Ward Beecher, Calvin Stowe, Theodore Dwight Weld, and Theodore Parker denounced the immorality of slavery. And women in larger numbers than ever before found a public outlet for their accepted roles as the guardians of morality in joining male abolitionists in the antislavery movement. Angelina and Sarah Grimké, who belonged to an aristocratic South Carolina family, Abby Kelley Foster, and Elizabeth Cady Stanton were but a few of the women who were prominent abolitionists. Still, during the antebellum period, the interest of middle-class women in reform generally was neither widespread nor was it significant in creating a vigorous program. In a nation where over 80 percent of the population still gained its livelihood from farming, women and men paid little or no attention to world peace movements, prison reform, or utopian communities.

Elizabeth Stanton and Lucretia Mott, women from upstate New York families, combined their abolitionist agitation with a campaign for women's rights. In 1848 at Seneca Falls, New York, they played a leading role in the first women's rights convention. They took the Declaration of Independence as their model for voicing their grievances against a male-dominated world, and proclaimed their intention to work for equality of the sexes.

Also present at the convention, where he electrified his audience of earnest women and a handful of male reformers, was the black abolitionist and orator Frederick Douglass. Douglass was a striking figure, over six feet tall, with an athletic build, bronzed features, and deeply creased forehead. Although he had had no formal education, Douglass possessed an extensive vocabulary. And he spoke in a cultured voice with an accent that he had taught himself to use in communicating with his audience. Born a slave in Maryland, the son of a black mother with Indian blood and a white father, Douglass had endured many vicissitudes in his early life, having been exposed to cruel, exacting masters as well as indulgent ones from whom he had learned to read and write. He had planned an escape when he was a young man, but his efforts were frustrated. In his second attempt, however, he had succeeded and made his way to New Bedford, Massachusetts, where he married and earned his living as a day laborer. Always studious, he had a passion for self-improvement. The scant leisure time he could spare he devoted to reading.

This extraordinary man became acquainted with William Lloyd Garrison, whose abolitionist journal *The Liberator* was staple reading material for the young fugitive black. When Garrison and other abolitionists saw how well-spoken he was and how quickly he developed a fine platform presence, they enlisted him in their cause. His first speeches, which were based on his own experience as a slave, were so vivid that they deeply moved his audience, even those who did not profess abolitionism. Indeed, some skeptics among those who listened to his accounts doubted their accuracy, prompting Douglass to publish a book in 1845 describing his experiences in detail and giving specific names, dates, and places. Entitled *Narrative of the Life of Frederick Douglass, An American Slave,* it became a popular work that sold 30,000 copies within the first five years of publication and catapulted Douglas to preeminence among black abolitionists. So candid were many of Douglass's comments that he feared he would be returned to slavery. As a result he fled the country for Great Britain. There he made an even greater impression than he had in Massachusetts. After two years abroad he returned to the

United States with ample funds to purchase his freedom and to establish an abolitionist newspaper, the *North Star*, in upstate New York. It was followed later by another publication, *Frederick Douglass's Weekly.*

Douglass's various periodicals were marked by highly intelligent and careful editing. They ranked with the very best of the abolitionist journals. And they were in general well supported, unlike most black papers, which fell victim to delinquent subscribers and insufficient financial backing. Despite these adverse conditions, over a score of black abolitionist papers and periodicals were published, primarily in urban centers from the mid-1830s until the outbreak of the Civil War. They contributed significantly to the multifaceted communication campaign of the antislavery forces in the North and were especially important in dispelling the myth of black social and racial inferiority.

Most black papers hewed to the single issue of emancipation, but Douglass's journals embraced an entire spectrum of reforms among which feminist causes held a high place. Another important cause that Douglass addressed was equal rights for blacks. Although slavery was generally considered to be a moral wrong in the free states, blacks there were still regarded as unfit to serve on juries, and in many northern states they were denied suffrage and other civil rights. In New York, for instance, male blacks had to own property worth at least $250 before they were permitted to vote. There was no property qualification for white voters. Ohio had a comprehensive set of so-called "Black Laws" that discriminated against blacks. Some were repealed in 1849 as a result of the efforts of Salmon P. Chase, but white suffrage and other racist laws were retained. Most northern states had Jim Crow laws or local ordinances that segregated the races.

Douglass differed from some black abolitionist leaders and most white reformers in his steadfast opposition to colonization. He viewed colonization as an even more deadly form of discrimination against native-born Americans. Colonization had been the earliest expression of antislavery protest in the new nation. Its proponents sought to encourage wide-scale emigration of the black population from the United States to Africa. In part colonization took its motivation from efforts of reformers, primarily those in the South, to reconcile the natural rights philosophy in the Declaration of Independence with the realities of racial adjustment in an overwhelmingly white society after emancipation. As late as 1827, the slave states had 130 colonization societies with 6,625 members as compared with only 24 societies with 1,500 members in the free states.

Southern statesmen like Henry Clay lent their prestige to the movement. But after it reached its high point in the South during the 1820s, the colonization movement went into a steep decline in that region while experiencing a corresponding acceleration in the North. The rapid expansion of cotton production in response to world demand and to technological advances in the cotton textile industry fixed more permanently the slave labor system in the South.

An impressive spokesman for emancipation and for equality of the races, the eloquent Philadelphian-born black Henry Highland Garnet, became an advocate of colonization after the founding of Liberia in western Africa. While most black abolitionists were not beguiled as Garnet was by the Liberian experiment, many of their white counterparts saw emigration to other areas in the world as a solution to the social problems they perceived in the wake of emancipation. Salmon P. Chase expressed a view, held privately by most free soilers, that different geographies were suitable for different races. "I have thought it not unlikely that the Islands of the West Indies and portions of South America would be peopled [by blacks] from the United States," he wrote Frederick Douglass, "that by them, civilization would be carried back to Africa, not under the colonization scheme, but of choice and free will." Needless to say Douglass rejected Chase's proposal. It was not until near the end of the Civil War that Abraham Lincoln and many other antislavery men abandoned colonization as a measure of public policy.

Yet the movement, however discriminatory and impractical, must be considered an aspect of a broader reform impulse that sought to focus on social questions and provide answers. Douglass, like Wendell Phillips, the Boston Brahmin, was one such reformer whose concerns went far beyond abolition and embraced a variety of causes that included not only civil rights but equality of opportunity irrespective of race or gender. But the public, especially in the North, was responsive not only to antislavery agitation but also to prohibition movements. The United States in the early years of the nineteenth century had become one of the heaviest alcohol-consuming nations in the Western world. With no restrictions on the distilling and the retailing of liquor and few community restraints on drinking, consumption of alcohol reached an annual rate of 7.1 gallons of alcohol for every male and female over fifteen years of age. Though drunkenness with its attendant social evils was most visible in the cities, it was common also in the countryside. As a result the temperance crusade popularized by Neal Dow, a Maine lawyer and politician, gained wide acceptance. Dow succeeded in getting the nation's first prohibition law on the statute books of his state in 1851. After 1830, as the Protestant clergy and other opinion leaders pushed prohibition, alcohol consumption dropped dramatically to about 5 gallons per capita in 1835, 3.1 in 1840, and 1.8 in 1850. The movement was so effective that by the 1840s the temperance lobby became an important political force on the state and local level. State after state began to adopt licensing laws that either taxed the sale of liquor or regulated its production.

Thus by 1860, through efforts of the Protestant clergy and the metropolitan dailies like the *New York Tribune* with its crusading editor, Horace Greeley, and its popular, weekly edition that circulated widely in the countryside, temperance, antislavery, and other reform movements were educating and persuading ever larger elements of the northern population. Politicians had been quick to capitalize on what they perceived to be popular trends and added an air of immediacy to certain reforms as they sought to enlist the votes of their constituencies. Conversely southern ministers, opinion leaders, and especially the politicians relied on oral persuasion, which was more effective in a region where illiteracy was far greater than in the North. These spokesmen projected a different message that was more personal, less intellectual in style and substance. The North, they claimed, would eventually abolish slavery and, what was more feared among the masses of credulous farmers, would enforce the social equality of the races.

The wellsprings of the reform movement that began in the early 1830s and that featured abolition, temperance, and cultural identity represented a concerted effort to cope with the underlying problems of a transitional society. Spurred on by religious revivalists in the North and South, preachers such as Charles Grandison Finney and Peter Cartwright, the reform movement soon took on a secular and political thrust which became regionalized as opinion leaders sought to define it in their own terms. Abolitionism broadened into the Free Soil movement and eventually into an organized political protest. Prohibition made similar headway in state politics. Like abolitionism and the beginning of a women's rights movement, prohibition sought to halt through legislation what was perceived to be the moral and social disintegration of traditional cultural values as the industrial revolution in full tide began to engulf the North and the Midwest and reach into the South. Even the South, while still clinging desperately to its slave-plantation system of social control and economic exploitation, was experiencing modernization's impact as the pace of railroad development accelerated there during the 1850s. Some southerners too, began to seek an American society where the anachronism of slavery would eventually be removed.

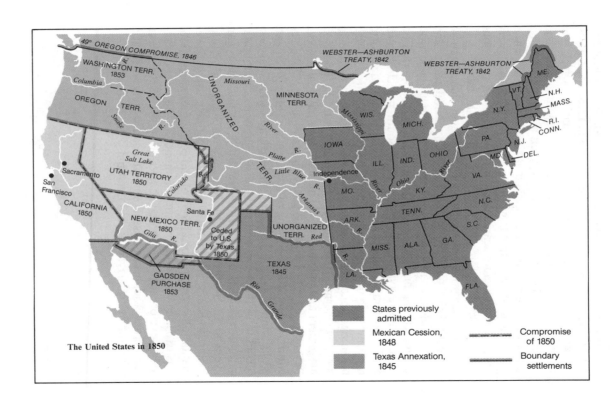

The United States in 1850

49° OREGON COMPROMISE, 1846

WASHINGTON TERR. 1853

Columbia *R.*

OREGON TERR.

Snake *R.*

UNORGANIZED

Missouri

MINNESOTA TERR.

WEBSTER—ASHBURTON TREATY, 1842

WEBSTER—ASHBURTON TREATY, 1842

ME.

VT.

N.H.

MASS.

N.Y.

R.I.

CONN.

WIS.

MICH.

PA.

N.J.

Great Salt Lake

UTAH TERRITORY 1850

Colorado *R.*

TERR.

Platte R.

Little Blue R.

Independence

IOWA

ILL.

IND.

OHIO

MD.

DEL.

VA.

San Francisco

Sacramento

Arkansas R.

MO.

KY.

CALIFORNIA 1850

NEW MEXICO TERR. 1850

Santa Fe

Ceded to U.S. by Texas 1850

UNORGANIZED TERR.

Red R.

ARK.

TENN.

N.C.

S.C.

Gila R.

GADSDEN PURCHASE 1853

TEXAS 1845

Rio Grande

MISS.

ALA.

GA.

LA.

FLA.

- States previously admitted
- Mexican Cession, 1848
- Texas Annexation, 1845
- — — — Compromise of 1850
- ——— Boundary settlements

CHAPTER TWO

A Temporary Armistice

As Van Buren prepared to turn over the presidency to Harrison in March 1841, the nation was still mired in the depths of a worldwide depression. It was moreover riven with sectional and class discontentment. But surely brighter days were ahead. A long-standing dispute with Great Britain over the border between the United States and Canada from Maine to the Rocky Mountains was on the verge of solution. And equally important to the future of the nation, Samuel F. B. Morse, a New England artist and amateur scientist, had invented the telegraph, which along with the railroad was to revolutionize communications in the Western world.

These developments aside, neither the abolitionists nor Calhoun's following took any comfort from the new President's stand on the slavery issue. The sixty-eight-year-old Harrison, in a tedious, rambling inaugural address, seemed to indicate that his administration would follow the same course on abolition that Van Buren had staked out. That is, a moderate policy where the executive branch would seek to assure the slave states it would not interfere with the institution where it existed and by implication would protect it wherever national power extended. But the address was so vague and so general on this area of public concern that no one could decide what if any direction President Harrison would take. Nor was he any more specific on other areas of policy like tariff, public lands, currency, or banks. Thurlow Weed's reaction was typical of Whig party leaders. "The inaugural does not meet expectations," he said. "It gives the administration no strength. . . . if Congress is called and does not carry out the measures required we are dished." And the Whigs, once they had gained office, proved as rapacious for political plums as the Democrats. Horace Greeley, who was observing the scene in Washington just before Harrison's inauguration, made these acid comments. "We have nothing here in politics, but large and numerous swarms of office-hunting locusts sweeping on to Washington daily. All the rotten land speculators, broken bank directors, swindling cashiers etc. etc. are in full cry for office, office. . . . my soul is sick of it."

Greeley's disgust with his party's behavior simply pointed out a new characteristic in American life, the professionalization of partisan politics. No longer could the opponents of Jacksonianism accuse it of degrading the political process. So-called republican virtue, disinterested public service for the benefit of the commonwealth, was now a thing of the past, a mere memory of a time when gentlemen of property and standing managed the government.

Tippecanoe, Tyler, and Texas

Despite the chagrin of idealists like Greeley and realists like Weed, contemporary observers, noting the composition of Harrison's cabinet and the direction of Whig leadership in Congress, were certain that Harrison would be a puppet in the powerful hands of Daniel Webster and Henry Clay. Webster as secretary of state would guide the nation's foreign policy, and it was felt that he would help determine Harrison's approach to domestic affairs. Webster would share power in this area with Henry Clay, who stood ready to enact his "American System" of a protective tariff, a third Bank of the United States, a federally financed and controlled system of internal improvements, and an inflationary monetary policy.

Harrison died, however, after one month in office, and the nation for the first time in its brief history was faced with a Vice President assuming the office of chief executive. This in itself would not have caused concern except that the new President, John Tyler, was not a Whig in the Clay or Webster mold. He was one of those curious Virginia politicians who in most respects followed the Democratic line but who had certain Whiggish tendencies. Whig party leaders had chosen him for just these qualities, which they thought would strengthen the ticket, especially in the South.

Tyler believed passionately in states' rights and other Jeffersonian ideals. But he had just as vehemently opposed the Jackson and Van Buren administrations on many policy matters. He thought nullification was an absurd abstraction, but he had voted against Jackson's measure that forced South Carolina to comply with the tariff law. He was known to favor federal distribution of public lands to the states, and he opposed the subtreasury system. His position on the currency question approximated Whig soft money policy, as did his stand on internal improvements. As a United States senator from 1827 to 1836 he had voted with Clay and Calhoun on the Compromise Tariff of 1833, but whether he would support another central bank under the sponsorship of the federal government was another question. Tyler's contradictory record on vital Whig measures had been brushed aside when Whig leaders sought a ticket in the campaign of 1840 which would appeal to the widest possible electorate. After all, it was assumed he would perform the innocuous role of Vice President and would be excluded from policy decisions.

The sudden death of Harrison exposed the folly of the Whig election strategy. For the next four years, Whig leaders saw the most important elements of their program of national planning frustrated by a stubborn President who did not share their policy views. Under Clay's leadership, the Whig majority in Congress approved a third Bank of the United States, which was considered essential to the party's program of economic recovery and industrial growth. When Tyler vetoed the bill and further efforts in Congress to meet his objections failed, all of the Harrison cabinet except Webster resigned in protest. Webster was deeply involved in negotiations with Great Britain over the boundary between Canada and the United States. He remained in office until he had successfully negotiated with Lord Ashburton, the British envoy, a definitive treaty. Although Tyler did approve Whig measures such as the repeal of the subtreasury act and the enactment of a protective tariff, the leaders read him out of the party. Nor would the Democrats accept him. For the remainder of his term Tyler sought vainly to create a third party through the executive patronage that he controlled. The political difficulties of the Harrison and Tyler administrations and the continuation of hard times deflected public attention briefly from the slavery issue.

But Tyler, in part because he wished to further his own political future, in part because of counsel he was receiving from Calhoun partisans in his cabinet, and in part because of a popular mood he sensed, opened up the Texas annexation issue that the previous administrations had sidetracked. Calhoun, now associating himself with the Democratic opposition, had become an active candidate for his party's nomination to the presidency. He too regarded Texas annexation as a popular issue, though his overriding concern was its importance for strengthening the slave states. Through his supporters in the cabinet, namely, Secretary of State Abel P. Upshur and Navy Secretary Thomas W. Gilmer, Calhoun guided the Tyler administration in its negotiations with Texas. A draft treaty of annexation had already been drawn up when in early 1844 Upshur and Gilmer were killed by the accidental explosion of a gun on the navy ship *Princeton*. Tyler then appointed Calhoun as Upshur's successor. Within a short time Calhoun had completed all negotiations with Texas and submitted a draft treaty to the Senate. But obsessed with his mission to protect the South and its slave-plantation system and incensed by the House repeal of the "gag rule" on abolitionist petitions, he sent along with the treaty his correspondence with the British minister, Sir Richard Pakenham, regarding Texas and abolitionism. Calhoun's correspondence was such a one-sided and strident defense of slavery that it became at once a political statement for southern extremists. Thus slavery and Texas annexation threatened to divide the Democratic party at its presidential nominating convention in 1844. It was little wonder that many northern congressmen gained a false impression of southern strength and feared an aggressive expansion of the slave-plantation system. John M. Niles, a senator from Connecticut during the Polk administration, was one of a growing group of northern politicians who fervently believed that free labor and free institutions were being encircled by an expansionist slave system, preparatory to the establishment of slavery everywhere in the Union. Before the outbreak of the Mexican-American War, Niles gave vent to fears that the annexation of Texas had aroused in the North. "We want Texas," he said, "but not at the expense of the Constitution. . . . to admit a state larger than all the territory northwest of the Ohio & give it the power of retaining its limits, or of carving out of them four states; and this to guarantee slavery, in advance in the whole country whether people who may settle it, desire it or not, is asking a little too much." Niles represented a group of capable politicians who would introduce the Wilmot Proviso to restrict slavery from the territory that might be gained as a result of a peace settlement with Mexico after the termination of hostilities.

Expansion and War with Mexico

Earlier Van Buren, the leading Democratic candidate, and Henry Clay, the prospective Whig nominee, had agreed to delay annexation until it could be accomplished without precipitating a war with Mexico. But the Calhoun-Pakenham correspondence together with public letters of support for annexation from Andrew Jackson and other leading Democratic politicians immediately made Texas a prime political issue. When Van Buren and Clay issued letters opposing annexation, both risked their party's nomination for the presidency. Van Buren was shelved at the Baltimore convention in favor of James K. Polk, former Speaker of the House and a Jackson protégé who favored immediate annexation. Henry Clay received the Whig nomination, but he had been forced to retreat from his former position on Texas and by election day had all but accepted annexation.

Another aspect of western expansion, settlement of the Oregon border with Great Britain, was also an issue in the campaign. The United States claimed a boundary line of 54° 40' north, which would have included about half of present day British Columbia and all of Vancouver Island. Britain insisted that the Columbia River was the southern boundary of its Canadian province. Under an agreement between the two nations signed in 1818, the territory was jointly occupied with a tacit understanding that United States' interests were predominant in the south, or present-day Oregon. Either nation could denounce the treaty after a one-year notice of its intention. Since the joint occupancy agreement, first American fur traders, notably those employed by John Jacob Astor and his American Fur Company, and then American settlers in greater numbers pushed into the territory south of the Columbia River. British fur traders, especially those of the Hudson's Bay Company, operated north of that informal line. By 1844 fur-bearing animals, primarily the beaver, had been so depleted in the Northwest that both British and American fur traders had shifted their interests elsewhere. But the American presence in the area had been strengthened as emigrants from the United States took up farms in Oregon and what is now southern Washington.

Population in this distant northwest territory grew slowly, however, isolated as it was from the settled areas of the Union. When the boundary emerged as a political issue in the early

1840s, the territory had less than 10,000 inhabitants. Yet Oregon became bound up with Texas annexation as the free states in the Midwest came to view the territory as a counterweight to the slaveholders' interest in Texas.

Westward expansion, always a compelling theme since the end of the Revolutionary War, had taken on new dimensions after the War of 1812 removed the last British and significant Indian barriers to westward migration. Rationalized and popularized by the young Irish-American editor of *The Democratic Review*, John L. O'Sullivan, the idea of territorial expansion, expressed in his term "Manifest Destiny," attached an emotional mystique to westward movement. O'Sullivan's editorials captured the imagination of Democratic party leaders in the South and West, though this ebullient national mood extended to all areas of the Union and was by no means merely a partisan or sectional expression. Skeptical of such emotional campaigns, Tyler's secretary of state Calhoun was primarily interested in the expansion of slave territory in the Southwest. But he also pushed energetically for a settlement in the Northwest that would satisfy American territorial aspirations. He had made considerable headway in his negotiations with Great Britain over the Oregon boundary before he left office on March 4, 1845.

Polk defeated Clay in the election of 1844 by the narrowest of margins. In fact, if the abolitionists had not offered a ticket in the campaign, Clay would have taken New York state and won the election. James G. Birney, running a second time as the Liberty party candidate, received over 60,000 votes, enough in several states to spell the margin of difference between the two major parties.

The new President sought to steer a course that would make his administration independent of the two party leaders, Calhoun and Van Buren. Calhoun, who had hoped to remain secretary of state, was replaced by James Buchanan, a party stalwart from the relatively neutral ground of Pennsylvania. Similarly, Polk brushed aside Van Buren's recommendations for major cabinet posts. Robert J. Walker, the expansionist senator from Mississippi, was made secretary of the treasury and William L. Marcy, now a political opponent of Van Buren in New York, was appointed secretary of war. So bitter had party strife become in the Empire State between the conservative faction (or the "Hunkers" as they were derisively called), and the "Barnburners", the more radical Van Buren group, that the Marcy appointment began the process of destroying Democratic party unity in New York and in other northern states. The appointment of the historian George Bancroft of Massachusetts, a man presumably close to Van Buren, to head the Navy Department did nothing to lessen a serious party division.

Polk's foreign policy in the short run was better conceived than his political appointments. Early on he had decided that besides the annexation of Texas, the United States must have a port on the Pacific coast. Frankly imperialistic, he had his eye on San Francisco. Before his administration was many months old, he sent a secret mission under the Louisiana lawyer-politician, John Slidell, to purchase California, what is now most of the territory comprising the states of New Mexico and Arizona, and all intervening territory that Mexico claimed south and west of the Louisiana Purchase line. For this cession Polk was willing to offer Mexico as much as $40 million. The Mexican government refused to receive Slidell, and from that point onward Polk resolved to acquire the territory even if it meant war with Mexico. He ordered the United States army commander in the Southwest, General Zachary Taylor, to move his small army westward to the Rio Grande. Hostilities between the two nations came about as a matter of course.

Taylor won a series of victories over the poorly led and wretchedly trained Mexican army. But the Polk administration found it politically necessary to strike at the heart of Mexico if it were to secure a satisfactory peace. Accordingly army chief General Winfield Scott led an expedition into central Mexico from the east. He also scored a series of victories, culminating with the capture of Mexico City. The administration's envoy,

Nicholas Trist, a state department official, managed to negotiate a peace treaty with the Mexican government that for a payment of $15 million secured a huge land cession of over a half-million square miles for the United States. The Treaty of Guadalupe Hidalgo that Trist negotiated included all of the present-day states of California, Utah, Nevada, a part of Colorado and Wyoming, and New Mexico and Arizona excepting only 45,000 square miles along the Gila River. (This border territory, acquired in the Gadsden Purchase of 1853, would be secured later for a transcontinental railroad route.) In addition, Mexico gave up all claims to the disputed territory of what is now western Texas and Oklahoma. Though Polk had disavowed his envoy, congressional opinion was such that he had no choice but to accept the treaty, which the Senate approved in May 1848.

Just before the Mexican-American war began, the Polk administration had settled the Oregon boundary with Great Britain. The President and Secretary of State James Buchanan had engaged in aggressive diplomacy. But they finally agreed to the present-day boundary of Washington state along the forty-ninth parallel. Thus in his single term as President, Polk had added about 33 percent to the land mass of the Union.

He had not accomplished this enormous territorial gain without opposition from the Whigs and from elements within his own party. Calhoun, speaking for the southern extremists, had opposed the war because he thought that such a huge acquisition of territory would imperil the Union. His fears were realized when in August 1846, David Wilmot, a Democratic congressman from Pennsylvania, moved an amendment to an appropriation bill that would exclude slavery from any territory that might be gained in a peace treaty with Mexico. His measure, modeled on the antislavery provision of Thomas Jefferson's Northwest Ordinance, passed the House of Representatives, where the free states had a clear majority. It was defeated in the Senate, however. The Proviso, which was repeatedly tacked on proposed legislation originating in the House, was invariably blocked in the Senate. The demand for free soil in those areas of the Union where congressional authority extended—the territories and the District of Columbia—had ceased to be simply an abolitionist cry and had become a political issue within both of the major parties.

Historians have considered James K. Polk to be near the first rank of American Presidents. After all, he increased the land mass of the nation by more than one-third and rounded out the contiguous territory of the continental United States. They also point to the undisputed fact that he announced his agenda at the beginning of his term of office and fulfilled it, something no other chief executive has ever accomplished. Polk stipulated that he would move the tariff in the direction of free trade; that he would reimpose the subtreasury system; that he would settle the Oregon and Texas boundaries; and that he would serve only one term in office. Actually with the Mexican cession he exceeded his announced program.

But at what cost? Politically, he had crippled the two-party system, opening the way for a sectional rearrangement of parties. By insisting on the acquisition of California and the New Mexico territory, he had helped shape the slavery question in such a way that it placed an unbearable strain on the nation's political integrity. There is little doubt that problems connected with the Mexican cession which were unforeseen when the Polk administration opted for war bore a direct connection to the constitutional and political crisis of 1860–1861.

Stalemate

Belatedly the Polk administration recognized the danger and sought to avert it. First it supported a plan that Stephen A. Douglas proposed. The northern boundary of Texas would be adjusted at 36°30′, the Missouri Compromise line. All the territory south of that line and westward to what is now the California border would be ceded to Texas. California would be admitted as a state. When Polk broached this idea to Calhoun, he met instant and vehement objection. Calhoun took particular exception to the admittance of California as a state because he claimed that slaveholders had been prevented from emigrating to it with their slaves and that as a result it would enter the Union as a free state.

Faced with decided opposition from Calhoun's following and from northern supporters of the Wilmot Proviso, Polk dropped this approach to the territorial problem. But the President tried again, this time without reference to the Texas boundary. Through Senator Jesse Bright of Indiana, Polk offered an amendment to the Oregon territorial bill that was before Congress. The amendment would extend the Missouri Compromise line to the Pacific and would apply it to all of the Mexican cession south of that line. Bright's amendment also contained a fugitive slave clause as a concession to southern extremists. Neither the free-soil element nor Calhoun's contingent would support the compromise measure, which failed on the floor of the Senate. The Senate did approve a compromise amendment which was reported from a select committee chaired by John M. Clayton of Delaware. This amendment, which provided for the admission of Oregon without the Wilmot Proviso and for the organization of territorial governments in California and New Mexico with a judicial settlement of the slavery issue there, was defeated in the House.

Following the administration's failure to find a compromise for the slavery issue, both Democratic and Whig politicians began in earnest to forestall what they perceived to be the perils that lay ahead. Daniel Dickinson, a Hunker senator from New York, proposed a solution to the problem which gained immediate favor from conservative Democrats both North and South. The Dickinson formula would deny congressional power over the territories in the matter of slavery and would assign it to actual residents. Labeled "popular sovereignty," this approach seemed superficially to be a democratic way of heading off a threatening situation. Lewis Cass, a Jacksonian Democrat from Michigan and a champion of western interests, gained the Democratic presidential nomination in

1848 by subscribing to popular sovereignty. In a public letter to A. O. P. Nicholson, a leading Tennessee politician, Cass not only accepted this formula but defended his position with an elaborate constitutional argument. Whig party leaders, hungry for office, shelved Henry Clay and Daniel Webster in favor of nominating another military hero, this time Zachary Taylor, a southerner and a slaveholder.

There were antislavery groups in both parties, but some able Van Buren Democrats who had pushed the Proviso were becoming the nucleus for a separate political organization. The cleavage in the party in New York state between the Hunkers and the Barnburners, which the Polk administration had widened, was evident at the Democratic convention that nominated Cass. A combination of antislavery sentiment and resentment of southern domination of the party prompted Van Buren to accept a third-party nomination on the Free Soil ticket. The elderly ex-President was quite explicit in expressing his views informally to visitors at Lindenwald, his home in upstate New York, and in public letters. On July 5, 1848, he told a departing guest who had become a Free Soiler, "young man, you have chosen a good part. Persevere to the end, which you may see, but I shall not. The recent aggressions of the slave power may destroy the old parties, but they will perpetuate the republic. You have enlisted under the banner of *Free Soil*, carry it forward to victory. The contest may be long. I foresee that it will not be ended by the present campaign. . . . Slavery cannot exist under restrictions. It must expand or perish."

Earlier Van Buren had accepted the Wilmot Proviso and argued that Congress held exclusive power over the territories. He also declared that the Founding Fathers had all condemned slavery and looked forward to its eventual abolition. In a severe arraignment of Calhoun's position, he charged that the South Carolinian's doctrine "therefore plainly states . . . wherever the flag of the Union goes, it carries slavery with it; it overturns the local institutions, no matter how strongly entrenched in the legislation, the habits and affections of the people, if freedom be their fortunate condition, and establishes in its place slavery." But Van Buren went beyond the constitutional and political limitations on the Union that the southern ultras were seeking to impose. He asserted that free white labor would never work together with slaves, an argument that appealed to the workers of the North but one which Calhoun had repeatedly insisted was certainly not the case in the South.

Whether either statesman was accurate in his stand on slave labor, Van Buren's comment made sense to the more pragmatic among the abolitionists who had been moving towards the realistic and constitutional goal of isolating slavery in the South, where local laws and customs protected it. Under the guidance of politically astute leaders in the Liberty party like Salmon P. Chase of Ohio and John P. Hale of New Hampshire, the antislavery movement now concentrated its energies and resources on prohibiting slavery in the territories. The Wilmot Proviso debates had strengthened the Free Soil advocates among the abolitionists and had opened the way for a merger with the Van Buren wing of the Democratic party.

Needless to say, the concept of popular sovereignty was anathema not only to these individuals, but also to extreme southern states' rights advocates. Shortly before his death, Calhoun denounced popular sovereignty as simply an abdication of all authority to an ill-defined group of transients. In an argument that foreshadowed the majority opinion in the Dred Scott case, he claimed that the Constitution gave Congress power to legislate for the territories, but that such legislation must protect slavery as property in accordance with the due process clause of the Fifth Amendment. Under this reasoning, the Northwest Ordinance, the Missouri Compromise, and the Wilmot Proviso were all unconstitutional.

Taylor won the election over Cass by a slight margin. The Van Buren vote had spelled the margin of difference in several crucial states. This manifestation of northern antislavery feeling, while still a distinct minority (Van Buren polled 290,000 votes out of more than 2,500,000 votes cast) was most disturbing to southern political leaders. They assumed, and correctly, that the Free Soil vote indicated a much deeper hostility turns. Determined defenders of slavery saw the beginnings of an ominous movement to isolate slavery as a preliminary move to abolishing the institution everywhere in the republic.

Several serious trials of strength between the two sections had already occurred in the closing days of the Polk administration. The House of Representatives voted to instruct its committee on territories to report a bill that would abolish the slave trade in the District of Columbia, only to rescind its action in the face of concerted southern opposition. But the most bitter debate arose over the Oregon territorial bill. The Wilmot Proviso had been attached to this proposed legislation. Only after protracted and bitter argument was it passed in both houses and received the President's signature.

California and Compromise

Meanwhile gold had been discovered in California and the new territory received a sudden, dramatic influx of population. The gold miners and other adventurers attracted to California's booming economy formed their own constitution that excluded slavery. They sought admission to the Union as a state without going through territorial status. These events, following so closely on the campaign of 1848, momentarily crystallized southern opinion in Congress. At a bipartisan meeting of representatives and senators from the slave states, it was decided to formulate and issue an address to the people of the South protesting perceived northern aggression against southern social and economic institutions. Calhoun was asked to draft the address. The result was an incendiary document that outlined a conspiracy on the part of the North to encircle and subjugate the South, destroying its slave-plantation society and empowering the emancipated slaves to be the rulers of the region. Conservative and moderate opinion in the North as well as the South was shocked at this harsh indictment. The Whig contingent of southern congressmen, at the urging of the new President, Zachary Taylor, refused to support Calhoun's position. Yet the address had considerable impact on public opinion, especially in the South. In Alabama, Florida, Virginia, and South Carolina conventions or legislative caucuses insisted that Congress had no power to restrict slavery in the territories. Responding to the pressure, Congress postponed consideration of bills that would create territorial organizations for California and New Mexico.

The focus of the public debate on territories now shifted to President Taylor. Though a southerner and a slave owner, Taylor had come under the influence of free-soil Whigs in his cabinet and in Congress. The new senator from New York, William H. Seward, was particularly persuasive. In the fall of 1849, Taylor sent T. Butler King, formerly a Whig congressman from Georgia and a moderate on the question of slavery in the territories, to California on a fact-finding mission. King reported back that public opinion in California overwhelmingly rejected slavery. The President accepted King's estimate of the situation and threw the administration's support behind the admission of California as a free state, bypassing the territorial stage that southern militants claimed Congress had to acknowledge in order to protect slavery. Taylor's action incensed extremists and moderates alike in the slave states. In October 1849 a bipartisan convention held at Jackson, Mississippi, called upon the slave states to send delegates to a convention which would be held at Nashville in June 1850. A month later the South Carolina legislature chose delegates to the convention. This action was followed by Alabama, Georgia, and Virginia, whose governors endorsed the Mississippi resolutions. When the Thirty-first Congress met on December 3, 1849, a separation of the southern states from the Union was a distinct possibility.

On hand was the old triumvirate of Calhoun, Clay, and Webster, all in precarious health, Calhoun actually only a few months from his deathbed. What he had striven for over the past twenty years—southern unity—seemed about to be achieved. But Calhoun hoped that the Union and the protection of the slave-plantation system within it could be preserved. Southern unity, as he saw it, was the means whereby the free states would be forced to concede lasting guarantees. He made himself plain on this burning issue in his last speech to the Senate. So weak that he had to have his remarks read for him by the Virginia senator James M. Mason, Calhoun presented the demands of the southern militants, which amounted to virtual autonomy, secured by constitutional amendment, for the slave states. Division among southern congressmen over the means to protect slavery in the territories, however, became apparent almost at once.

Henry Clay had already offered a series of bills that might form the basis of a compromise—a strengthened fugitive slave law, settlement of Texas's western boundary, assumption of the Republic of Texas's debt, abolition of the slave trade in the District of Columbia, California to be admitted as a free state, New Mexico organized as a territory with neither the Wilmot Proviso nor any mention of slavery. Clay was appealing to the moderates north as well as south and he counted on help from the many in Congress who had purchased Texan bonds to vote for the package, or the "Omnibus bill" as it was called.

On March 7, 1850, Webster threw his prestige and his oratorical abilities behind the compromise measures. It was at this point that Calhoun despaired of the Union and made his prediction that it would cease to exist within the next ten to twelve years. Like Calhoun, President Taylor opposed Clay's compromise, though for completely opposite reasons. He was insistent that California be admitted at once as a free state with no strings attached. And he made it plain that if the South resisted he would lead the army personally against the region. Taylor's death in the summer of 1850, which followed that of Calhoun by a scant three months, removed the two imposing obstacles to a truce between the sections.

Behind the scenes, Stephen A. Douglas, the agile Democratic senator from Illinois, managed adroitly to draw together the fragmented majority that was for compromise. Douglas was an archetypical westerner, though a New Englander by birth and upbringing. At thirty-seven, he was the youngest man in the United States Senate. He had moved west in 1833 and established himself as a lawyer in Illinois, where he soon built up a lucrative practice. He had the massive head and torso of a tall, muscular man joined to stubby legs. He was scarcely five feet tall, but seemed a much larger person. Highly articulate, supremely self-confident, Douglas was at his best in the cut and thrust of the political arena. He was the ideal person to construct a winning coalition for the compromise measures. In this effort he was assisted by the new President, Millard Fillmore, who as Vice President had presided over the compromise debates in the Senate. A conservative Whig, Fillmore exerted all of the influence at his command to bring about the consensus Douglas was seeking. By September 1850, after months of debate which frequently became rancorous, the Compromise of 1850 was reached. President Fillmore signed the various bills and the Union was preserved for another decade.

Debate over the Compromise dampened enthusiasm that had been building up in the South for the Nashville Convention. Of the nine southern states that sent delegates, only those from South Carolina and Mississippi were for extreme measures if California were admitted as a free state. Moderates controlled the committee on resolutions, which in general supported the efforts of the compromisers in Washington. The most significant stand was a reaffirmation of the Missouri Compromise line with respect to new territories. An extremist measure threatening secession on the California issue passed, but only after strenuous opposition. Though it failed to unite the South on the slavery issue, the convention did provide a forum for radicals and to a considerable extent crystallized anti-Union sentiment throughout the slave states.

In the aftermath of the convention militant southerners made concerted attempts to effect joint action against the Compromise. And for a time disunion sentiment ran strong in the Deep South. But a combination of high cotton prices that brought prosperity to the slave states and a well-conceived Unionist movement frustrated the extremists. Secession, however, as an alternative to any public policy that threatened the existing social order in the South still commanded a majority opinion in the region.

The North, on the other hand, resented deeply the fugitive

slave law as an abrogation of state power, due process, and human rights. For the law denied a fugitive access to the state courts and prohibited him from giving testimony or evidence in his own behalf. A fugitive slave law had been on the federal statute books since 1793. The Constitution, in Article IV, section II, contained a fugitive slave provision that seemed to place the burden of identification and return upon both federal and state authorities. But the provision and the law that flowed from it were general in nature, and as a result were subject to varying interpretations. As early as 1824 northern states began passing what were termed "personal liberty laws." Some legislation positively forbade either the federal government or a state to return a fugitive within their boundaries to slavery. Other laws insisted on jury trials to determine the status of the fugitives. A Pennsylvania statute of 1826 made it also a felony akin to kidnapping for an individual to seize a fugitive and return him to slavery.

In 1842, however, the Supreme Court in the celebrated case of *Prigg* v. *Pennsylvania* declared that particular personal liberty law unconstitutional. In a reaffirmation of judicial nationalism, Associate Justice Joseph Story, who wrote the majority opinion, held that the extradition of a fugitive was exclusively a federal power. Story had gone against other nationalists from his own region of New England like Daniel Webster, who held that the fugitive slave provision in the Constitution rested on comity between the states. Webster and others who were dissatisfied with the *Prigg* decision pointed out that the particular section of the Constitution in which the fugitive slave clause appeared dealt exclusively with state power. It may have seemed paradoxical that Webster, who so often agreed with Marshall and Story in their broad interpretation of national powers, should in this instance have resorted to a states' rights position. On the other hand, southerners, even those of the extreme states' rights school of Calhoun, found fugitive slave cases convenient for enhancing federal power. But such was the case in this interesting development of the antislavery controversy. Nor was the legal assault by northern states on the fugitive slave issue abated with the *Prigg* case. The law in the Compromise of 1850 provoked northern lawyers and editorial writers to develop further Constitutional arguments which were embodied in a rash of new personal liberty laws. Charles Sumner, a Free Soiler and later a Republican senator from Massachusetts, defended his state's law by arguing that the Fugitive Slave Law deprived an escaped slave of procedural rights found in the Fifth, Sixth, and Seventh Amendments to the Constitution, and also deprived such a person of habeas corpus.

In addition to the fugitive slave controversy neither southern nor northern opinion was satisfied by the popular sovereignty feature of the Compromise that determined the organization of the vast New Mexico territory. Fears of northern aggression paralleled fears of southern encirclement and eventual destruction of free institutions. Knowledgeable politicians from both the free and the slave states realized that only an armistice, not a permanent and enduring peace, was in effect.

The period from 1837 to 1852 was a stormy political interlude where mounting sectional tensions were being voiced in debate over the future of the republic. They were also years during which the industrialization of the North had reached a takeoff point, while the southern states were increasingly rationalizing the slave-plantation system. Modes of cotton production were being improved on larger, more efficient plantations, which were beginning to profit from the large volume of production and the exploitation of rich bottom lands around the Mississippi delta that extended into western Louisiana and eastern Texas. Despite generally low prices for cotton that persisted from 1837 through the late 1840s in the world market, planters continued to bring more virgin lands into production. And in the old cotton states along the Atlantic seaboard, efforts were being made to combat erosion, drain swamps, and apply fertilizer to abandoned fields. South Carolina planters like Francis Pickens and James Henry Hammond were restoring land and improving production methods.

By 1850 the prosperity unleashed by the Mexican-American War, the discovery of gold in California, and the general air of confidence that peace and westward expansion bred had revived the domestic cotton market. Events in Europe, particularly the repeal of the Corn Laws by the British Parliament and the opening of its home market to American commodities, improved the balance of trade between the United States and Great Britain. American agricultural products and other raw materials were thus tied to the economic future of the British Empire, a future that was on the threshold of rapid expansion.

All of these positive market developments helped bring about a brief respite from sectional tension that enabled the politicians to put together the Compromise of 1850. Prosperity also ushered in a further expansion of the railroad network in the free states and the beginning of a notable development of a southern railroad system. But it seems likely that southern tardiness in modernization contributed to the sense of isolation, cultural difference, and rural provincialism that was decidedly more pronounced in the cotton states.

A Prophetic Statement

Essentially it was the institution of slavery with its associated social values that was defining and consolidating the cultural differences between the sections. The Wilmot Proviso and the rancorous divisions in Congress over California and Oregon were startling and ominous episodes in what was fast becoming a national debate over the future of the Union. The Free Soil campaign of 1848 injected for the first time a serious note of sectionalism that was threatening the existence of a national two-party system. Before the Free Soil schism of 1848, Whigs and Democrats irrespective of where they competed for office or how they presented their program each subscribed to a particular set of general principles. But the party battles of the Jacksonian period—the Bank, the tariff, and federal land policy—had now ceased to be hotly debated public questions. Gideon Welles, editor and formerly ardent Democrat, thought that the two major parties had become "mere hulks in the channel of progress." "They are," he predicted, "both to be brushed aside, for the honest instincts . . . of all the free states are right on the fugitive slave law, and freedom in the territories." The national party system that had existed in one form or another since the adoption of the federal Constitution was weakening and in another four years would begin to break down. Sectional political arrangements would replace the old parties. The North's antislavery sentiment and its mounting dedication to industrialism and free labor was even then challenging the peculiar institution on moral grounds and signaling that the future of the nation would be shaped by individual enterprise. These forces in the North regarded slavery as an anachronism and a contradiction of natural rights as expressed in the Declaration of Independence. William H. Seward gave voice to the forces that were undermining the major parties. In his carefully prepared address opposing the 1850 Compromise measures, this mainline Whig made a passionate plea for free soil when he said, "But there is a higher law than the constitution, which regulates our authority over the domain . . ."

Shortly before his death on March 31, 1850, John C. Calhoun made a prophetic statement. He said that the federal Union would be destroyed within the next generation: "I fix its probable occurrence within twelve years or three presidential terms. . . . the probability is, it will explode in a presidential election." What Calhoun had seen with startling clarity, and well before any of his contemporaries, was the likelihood of an impending division. While he did not describe the particular circumstances that prompted his fateful statement, he understood that irreconcilable tensions were building and that these would emerge in a political crisis that could result only in separation.

Calhoun had spent the last years of his life seeking to build a sectional coalition against northern aggression upon fundamental southern values. As he saw it, only a unified South could aggregate sufficient political power to halt the northern onslaught. And in the following years more and more southern politicians had come around to Calhoun's view of unified action. In fact, plans were well advanced to hold a southern convention when Calhoun died. What might have precipitated a disruption of the Union—the political future of the vast land mass obtained in the Mexican cession—was averted through the combined efforts of national political leaders in the Compromise of 1850. The compromise, however, was but a temporary truce in the contest between the sections.

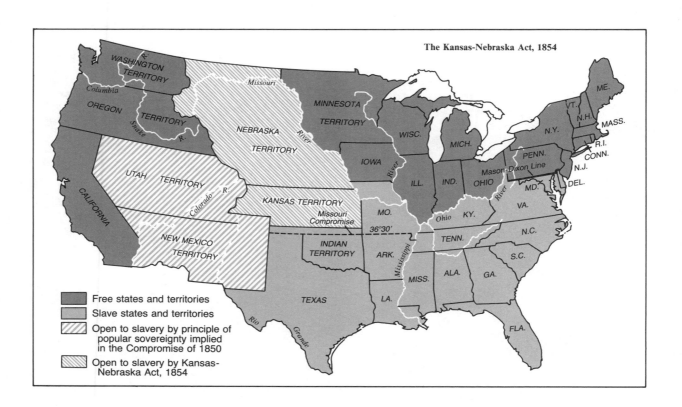

The Kansas-Nebraska Act, 1854

Legend:
- Free states and territories
- Slave states and territories
- Open to slavery by principle of popular sovereignty implied in the Compromise of 1850
- Open to slavery by Kansas-Nebraska Act, 1854

WASHINGTON TERRITORY

OREGON TERRITORY

Columbia R.

Snake R.

Missouri River

MINNESOTA TERRITORY

NEBRASKA TERRITORY

WISC.

MICH.

IOWA

River

ILL.

IND.

OHIO

N.Y.

PENN.

Mason-Dixon Line

ME.

VT.

N.H.

MASS.

R.I.

CONN.

N.J.

DEL.

MD.

UTAH TERRITORY

CALIFORNIA

Colorado R.

NEW MEXICO TERRITORY

KANSAS TERRITORY

Missouri Compromise

MO.

36°30'

Ohio

KY.

VA.

River

TENN.

N.C.

S.C.

INDIAN TERRITORY

ARK.

Mississippi

MISS.

ALA.

GA.

TEXAS

LA.

Rio Grande

FLA.

CHAPTER THREE

Kansas, First Phase

Once the crisis created by the Mexican cession had passed, confidence in the future of the nation returned. California gold and renewed demands for cotton and other commodities in northern and European markets stimulated the economy and brought about a renewed prosperity which was reflected in a buoyant national mood. Abundant cheap labor was flowing into northern mills and forges from a flood of European immigrants that the potato famine had displaced. Not all of these individuals settled for menial jobs in the factory towns and cities or along railroad construction routes of the North. Many migrated further west, adding their numbers and their productivity to the farm population.

Crop failures in Europe were not the only impulse to immigration. The liberal revolutions that swept over Europe in 1848 and their severe repression by autocratic governments, especially in the German states, sent a wave of political refugees, mainly educated and articulate individuals from the middle class, to the United States. Displaced immigrant farmers, peasants, and middle-class townfolk tended to avoid the South for economic and social reasons. Irish immigrants could not compete with slave labor in southern agriculture. Factory and railroad construction jobs were scarce in the region. German "forty-eighters" found slavery ideologically distasteful. Moreover they preferred the urban society that was more prevalent in the North than in the South. The sudden influx of an alien population created serious social problems in the cities of the North and West, whose institutions were completely inadequate to handle the newcomers. Nativism became an instant political issue as party leaders addressed themselves to the changes being wrought in society.

The boom in the cotton markets made the European carrying trade so profitable that heavy capital investments poured into shipbuilding and in the northern shipping industry. No symbol better characterized the expansive spirit of the mid-1850s than the graceful clipper ships, a product of Yankee design and mechanical ingenuity that set new speed records in the Atlantic and Pacific carrying trade. Politicians quickly sensed the national spirit and sought to capitalize on it for their own and their region's welfare. Even those militant northerners and southerners who had found in the Free Soil campaign a means of furthering their own careers by either defending or attacking slavery, seemed content to abide by the armistice of 1850.

Abolition and free soil, while still very much alive, for the time being had been moved aside in favor of railroad development, resumed speculation in western lands, a resurgence of capital investment in the slave-plantation economy and in northern industrial growth. "Young America" as a slogan had replaced "Manifest Destiny" in Democratic party circles, and proved even more attractive to the entrepreneurial instincts of the new western states. Stephen A. Douglas, the "Little Giant" as he was called, now a senator from the rapidly growing state of Illinois, personified western optimistic dedication to economic growth. Characteristically Douglas was reinforcing that image by serving as chairman of the Senate Committee on Territories and as a power in the Democratic party.

Whig Disintegration

The Whig party, whose great leaders Webster and Clay had lent their names and reputation to the Compromise of 1850, paradoxically became victim of its success in averting a disruption of the Union. On two major issues, slavery and territorial expansion, the Whig stance had become controversial, while the Democrats seemed to have been far more consistent. The Whigs had opposed the Mexican-American War and had gone against majority opinion, especially in the South. Taylor's stubborn insistence on admitting California as a free state and his apparent ties to Seward and other free-soil Whigs in his cabinet made party leadership most suspect to southern militants and moderates alike.

Other perceptions of the party—its elitist persuasion, its lack of a precise party doctrine—compared unfavorably with the vague but persistent notion of equality that the Democrats promoted and which found favor with the electorate. Whig ideas on fostering industrial development were portrayed by Democratic politicians as a concerted attempt to build up manufacturing at the expense of agriculture, whether it be cotton plantations worked by slave labor or farms everywhere in a predominately agrarian economy. The average farmer, who measured his living standard in terms of the price of wheat and corn and cotton, could be easily persuaded that protective tariff policies brought down the price of farm commodities in the world market, which in turn lowered the value of his product in the domestic market. In a nation whose transportation and communication links were as yet unformed, the Whig program of national planning was too advanced for the actual state of the economy to satisfy local aspirations. The economic argument for states' rights, emphasizing individual enterprise and local development, was far more consonant with the actual condition of the nation. Democratic politicians pointed to their subtreasury banking system and laissez-faire policies as the major reasons for the prosperous times that had existed since 1846. Certain prestigious present-day economists and economic historians who support free enterprise explanations have pointed to this period of continuous economic growth as proof of the vitality of marketplace capitalism. The federal government, the largest source of liquid capital in the nation, did indeed withdraw its financial support completely from the private sector after 1845. The reason for the nation's growth, however, can be best explained not by ideological arguments but rather by noting a key sequence of historic events. First, the Mexican-American War forced the government to relinquish part of its hoard of specie for military expenditures. Second, just as the war ended, the California gold rush poured millions of dollars of bullion into private channels. Third, when the influx of California gold waned in the mid-1850s, crop failures and the Crimean War in Europe stimulated enormously the world market for American commodities, again enriching the private sector and providing surplus capital for economic growth. Fourth, the cotton market that shared in the dramatic rise in American exports and that contributed mightily to a favorable trade balance during the period brought about an expansion of shipbuilding, which provided jobs and spread its economic bounty throughout the many subsidiary industries that were dependent upon it. The growth of American commerce that stemmed from the rising prosperity of commodities in the export market acted to earn foreign exchange and to provide the private sector with yet another means of expansion despite the deflationary impact of the subtreasury policy. When most of these factors ceased to operate, the panic and Depression of 1857 struck the economy of the industrializing northern states and brought about severe curtailment in production.

Economic issues aside, the Whig party as a national institution was as deeply beset by factionalism as its partisan rival. The political situation in New York state was a useful example of the differing fortunes of the Democratic and Whig parties. Barnburners and Hunkers, formerly warring factions of the Democratic party, had temporarily buried the hatchet there and elsewhere, though dissension still existed and menaced the political integrity of the incoming Pierce administration. Rivalry between the Seward and the Fillmore Whigs in the Empire State, however, had risen to a peak intensity and extended itself to other states in the Northeast and Midwest. This deeply felt internal animosity was destroying the party's national organization.

Seward and his political partner, Thurlow Weed, led a large and influential group of northern Whigs in opposition to the Compromise. In effect they split Whig integrity in the North and at the same time drove many southern Whigs into the Democratic party. In the South particularly, Whigs simply lost confidence in their party's national organization during the Compromise debate. Had Fillmore been a vigorous and adroit leader, he might have healed the wounds in his party and utilized the power and prestige of the presidency to bridge over the widening chasm between its northern and southern wings. But Fillmore was neither vigorous nor adroit. In fact, his failure to grasp the euphoric national mood after the Compromise stigmatized the Whig party as an ineffectual guardian of American interests. When, for instance, Spanish authorities executed American participants in a filibustering expedition in Cuba without protest from the United States government, the incident was cited as a prime example of Whig timidity when compared with the strident diplomacy of a Jackson or a Polk.

Whig weakness had been vividly demonstrated in the campaign and election of 1852. The Democrats again moved away from their experienced but controversial leaders like James Buchanan, Stephen A. Douglas, Lewis Cass, and William L. Marcy and selected Franklin Pierce, an attractive but pliable politician from New Hampshire and a lesser Mexican-American War hero of sorts. Winfield Scott, able general but a man whose appearance and personality quirks opened him

American War hero of sorts, Winfield Scott, able general but a man whose appearance and personality quirks opened him up to easy political caricaturing, was chosen as the Whig candidate. The national Democratic organization proved sound enough to withstand any sizeable defections.

In the campaign all of the sectional antagonisms the Compromise had provoked—the Fugitive Slave Law, abolition of the slave trade in the District of Columbia, admission of California as a free state—were blamed on the Whigs of the Seward-Weed stripe, while the Democrats claimed credit for averting a breakup of the Union. Pierce overwhelmed Scott in the electoral vote, 254 to 42. The Whigs carried only four states: Vermont, Massachusetts, Kentucky, and Tennessee. Support for the Free Soil party, which had taken 10 percent of the popular vote in 1848, was reduced significantly. John P. Hale, its presidential candidate, polled about 5 percent of the popular vote. Former Free Soilers such as Martin Van Buren and John M. Niles supported Pierce. Salmon P. Chase of Ohio called himself an "independent" Democrat. Southern politicians like Jefferson Davis, who had opposed the Compromise in the Congress and openly talked of disunion, softened their criticisms and backed the Democratic ticket. Clearly the country was in no mood to reopen sectional discord. But all was not well beneath a surface political calm. Extremists on both sides of the slavery issue were determined to maintain their position. Confident of an eventual breakup, they strengthened their respective organizations and bided their time.

Young America

Paradoxically, it was the very spirit of business confidence and entrepreneurial activity that touched off the explosion and began a realignment of parties on a sectional basis. In the spirit of "Young America," continental-minded community leaders, speculators, and politicians both north and south pushed for government support of railroads that would link the Far West to the Union. Government aid for improving and extending transportation and communication had been a political and constitutional issue since the formation of the United States in 1789. It had taken on a new significance after the War of 1812, when such nationalists as John C. Calhoun, Henry Clay, and John Quincy Adams had proposed internal improvement programs on a truly imperial scale. The National Republicans and their successors, the Whigs, had openly espoused Henry Clay's "American System" of massive government aid for turnpikes, canals, and railroads. While sympathetic to internal improvements, Democrats generally favored local development and control. But by the 1850s, it became clear to both parties that interstate ventures requiring large capital investments that transcended local interests were beyond the resources of individual states and their conflicting aspirations. Federal ownership of millions of acres of unsettled land was now looked upon as a source for financing extensive railroad ventures. The more densely populated eastern seaboard states already had an extensive railroad, road, and canal network, though the region south of Virginia still remained largely underdeveloped in this regard. Southwestern cotton states—Alabama, Mississippi, Texas, and Louisiana—continued to enjoy cheap transportation by utilizing the Mississippi River and its tributaries. But they too were not indifferent to the flexibility and convenience of railroad transport.

Yet it was natural that the center of agitation for government support came from the newer states of the West, including the border slave states, which were gaining rapidly in population and even more in expectations. The direction of federal land policy had been in contention since the creation of the republic. The outstanding achievement of the Confederation period had been the cession to the central government of most of the western territories which the states had claimed. Warrants for transfer of land up to 1100 acres were issued to Revolutionary War veterans in what would become a fixed policy. But most of these warrants for veterans of the Revolutionary War and the War of 1812 had fallen into the hands of speculators. Other large land grants had been made to groups like the Ohio Company in southeastern Ohio after Indian titles had been extinguished either by outright seizure or the purchase in scores of Indian treaties. The Louisiana and Florida purchases, the Mexican cession, and other territorial acquisitions boosted the area of federal lands to almost 2.5 million square miles. By 1855 land the government had distributed by military bounty to veterans of the Revolutionary War, the War of 1812, and the Mexican-American War exceeded 68 million acres. Besides military bounty lands, several huge grants had been made to questionable land companies, the largest and most spectacular being the Yazoo fraud in Georgia's western territories.

But the federal government throughout the period retained most of the public domain and at the insistence of the undeveloped West evolved a policy whereby its land holdings were utilized for actual settlement or distributed to the states for their disposal or for the encouragement of public works of general benefit like railroads, canals, turnpikes, and educational institutions. Beginning with the land law of 1796 that set up land offices and established tract sizes and modes of payment, Congress from then on spent a good deal of its time considering land policy. Western interests, anxious for the rapid development of their section, pressed for liberalization of federal land policy. Free land for homesteads was one of their objectives that eventually became law in 1862. A liberal land policy, however, was not secured without heated debate which took on both political and sectional overtones. The immediate cause for the famous Webster-Hayne debates in 1830 was sectional rivalry between the Northeast, the Southeast, and the West. During the quarter century between 1829 and 1854, a land policy evolved that was rife with partisanship and increasingly became involved in the contest over slavery.

Western interests, championed by Thomas Hart Benton, pushed for reforms of federal land policy. In the course of his arguments, Benton urged what he called "preemption," or the granting to squatters of options to purchase federal lands, and "graduation," which would reduce the price over a period of time for unsettled and unclaimed public land. Henry Clay added a third concept, "distribution," whereby the surplus revenue that the government obtained from the sale of public lands would be paid to the states in proportion to their representation in Congress. Clay's proposal came at a time when the treasury of the United States enjoyed a surplus. Thus it excited opposition even from westerners like Benton, who saw distribution as a ruse to keep the treasury bare so that tariffs could be raised under the pretext of revenue need. During the Polk administration distribution had become such an object of partisan rivalry that direct grants to new states as they came into the Union became fixed policy. Western demands for graduation and preemption persisted, however, and came to be supported by both Whig and Democratic administrations. Various acts embodying these principles evolved into general policy by 1862.

Still the most important land policy continued to be cessions to corporations. After 1850 grants in favor of railroad construction became the accepted means of furthering transportation in the public domain, and through them the fostering of settlement. Homestead bills, favored by such proto-populist politicians as Andrew Johnson from the hill country of eastern Tennessee and generally by Whig leaders from the West like Abraham Lincoln, were held up by southern and eastern interests until the Civil War.

Stephen A. Douglas, that apostle of western development, was in the forefront of the railroad entrepreneurs who were pushing for land grants. While he was negotiating the details of the Compromise of 1850, Douglas managed to push through Congress a bill that granted the Illinois Central Railroad 2,595,000 acres of land along its surveyed route south. Railroad land grants, which took their form from the Northwest Ordinance, allocated alternate sections of land to railroads with the assumption that these sections would help finance construction and at the same time stimulate settlement along the route. The Illinois Central precedent inaugurated a frenzy of special interest groups that besieged the Congress and made Douglas's Senate Committee on Territories one of the most important instruments of government. But beyond the unseemly competition of individual and community lobbyists were the various propositions for transcontinental routes. No sooner had the political and constitutional crisis of 1850 been averted than proponents of the transcontinental railroads descended on Washington with their claims. Of the many routes discussed, those moving westward from Chicago to San Francisco and the Pacific Northwest vied with those which had their eastern termini in St. Louis, Memphis, or New Orleans.

Douglas was well placed to push his own personal and regional interests. The geographic position of Chicago, favored by the Great Lakes and the Erie Canal that linked it with the populous East and by its proximity to the Mississippi River system and hence to the South, gave the bustling city an impressive advantage over other would-be competitors. So confident was Douglas in the economic future of Chicago that he had invested heavily in Chicago real estate and in large tracts of land further west in Minnesota Territory.

But southern interests also had an able advocate in a strategic position. Jefferson Davis, a graduate of West Point, a trained lawyer, Mexican War veteran, and Mississippi politician, was now Secretary of War in the Pierce administration. Quite naturally Davis favored a southern route from New Orleans through the Gila River valley to the port of San Diego in California. Davis and other southerners managed to have Congress appropriate funds to survey this southern route. The survey indicated that the most feasible route lay through Mexican territory just south of the New Mexico Territory. James Gadsden, a southern railroad promoter, was sent to Mexico with instructions to purchase the necessary land. He succeeded in negotiating a treaty. For $10 million, the United States secured about 45,000 square miles of territory. The treaty was pending when the Thirty-third Congress convened on December 5, 1853. Though it encountered spirited opposition, the Senate finally confirmed the treaty by a narrow margin.

The Kansas-Nebraska Bill

Meanwhile Douglas, seeking to capitalize on what he took to be widespread support for the popular sovereignty principle embodied in the Compromise of 1850, began the process of organizing the territory west of Missouri and Iowa, known collectively as the Nebraska Territory. Douglas was well aware of the political divisions that were already distracting the Pierce administration. The youthful President had been unsuccessful in harmonizing former Free Soil elements with mainstream Democrats through the patronage process. Douglas grasped what he thought was an opportunity to heal a growing schism in the party, placate expansive western interests, and seize the initiative from the President through a practical test of popular sovereignty. Yet he was concerned about the effect popular sovereignty would have on the Missouri Compromise if the principle were applied to the Nebraska Territory, which lay north of the Compromise line established for the Louisiana Purchase lands. He knew that northern opinion had canonized the Missouri Compromise and any trifling with that solemn covenant would, in his own words, raise "a hell of a storm."

The popular sovereignty idea embodied in the Compromise of 1850 applied only to the New Mexico Territory, a part of the Mexican cession that had not been part of the Union when Congress drew the Missouri Compromise line. But if the principle meant anything, and Douglas had staked his political future on it, then this technicality would pose no serious obstacle, because he believed that slavery could not exist in the arid Southwest. He wrote Howell Cobb, at the time a moderate southern Democrat and political supporter, that popular sovereignty "will triumph and impart peace to the country and stability to the union." He was confident that when the people came to understand his position they would support it, present criticism notwithstanding. Douglas reasoned that "the great principle of self government is at stake, and surely the people of this country are never going to decide that the principle upon which our whole republican system rests is vicious and wrong." Ever the careful politician, Douglas would not raise the Missouri Compromise issue. In the Nebraska bill which he drafted, he simply ignored that venerable geographic division between slave and free territory. In this way he hoped to avoid any political uproar. But he had misjudged the political climate and woefully misunderstood the extent of mutual fears and cultural differences between the two sections that slavery had so magnified.

Almost immediately southern politicians demanded that Douglas make an explicit repeal of the Compromise of 1820 in his bill. An early earnest of their intent came from a caucus of southern senators composed of both Whigs and Democrats. The caucus voted unanimously to support the bill, but made it unmistakably clear that it favored repeal of the Missouri Compromise, charging that the North had never abided by its provisions. These southern politicians cared little for the legal status of Louisiana Territory or the Mexican cession. Robert Toombs, formerly a Whig politician but now a Douglas Democrat from Georgia, wrote that "in the long struggle for gov'mts for California and N. Mexico the whole North, (with I think but four exceptions,) . . . repudiated and refused the Missouri Compromise." Toombs and many of his southern colleagues insisted that the Missouri Compromise was but a sectional arrangement, largely supported by southern votes. The Compromise of 1850 and its popular sovereignty principle, on the other hand, was a compact recognized by a majority in the North and adopted by both parties north and south in their party platforms.

At first Douglas resisted the pressure, but all along he felt trapped by his own public position on popular sovereignty, the obligation he felt he owed to his constituents, and by his own personal interests in the development of the trans-Mississippi West. Finally he believed that the northern prairies of the territory were not conducive to slavery. In a second draft of the bill, he followed the guidelines of the Compromise of 1850 and established popular sovereignty for the new territories, thus implicitly repealing the Missouri Compromise.

The southern bloc wanted more than that, however, for its assistance in passing the bill. Its representatives made it plain to Douglas that any territorial organization for Kansas and Nebraska must explicitly repeal the Missouri Compromise.

Word of these negotiations had of course reached the White House. The President and his cabinet were all of the opinion that the Missouri Compromise was an unconstitutional extension of congressional authority. But they differed on the means for removing it from the statute books. Their differences reflected sectional sympathies. The President and the northern members of his cabinet favored Douglas's original bill that ignored the Compromise. They were certain that if the matter were left to the Supreme Court, the Missouri Act would be declared unconstitutional. Thus the Democratic party would be spared a deep and threatening wrangle between its northern and southern wings. Southern members of the cabinet may have objected but finally agreed to an amendment that neither repealed nor completely ignored the Missouri Compromise and that declared that the Supreme Court was the appropriate authority to decide its constitutionality.

Although the Pierce administration's amendment was vague in meaning and imprecise in language, Douglas accepted it. Not so the more extreme southern Democratic leadership. In the most fateful decision of his life and that of the Union, Douglas bowed to their arguments. He had to act quickly as the bill was on the calendar for the next day's session. He felt he had to have the administration's sanction for explicit repeal, but the day was Sunday and he knew that Pierce transacted no business on the Sabbath. Enlisting the assistance of Jefferson Davis, Pierce's Secretary of War, Douglas secured an interview. Accompanied by Davis and by the five insistent southern senators, Douglas presented their collective decision to the President. Like Douglas before him, Pierce gave in and even agreed to formalize his agreement in writing, thus making the revised bill an administration measure. Still concerned about the political implications of the measure, the worried President asked that his secretary of state, William L. Marcy, the old party veteran from New York, be consulted. But Marcy was not available and as time was of the essence, the revised bill came up for debate on Monday, January 23, 1854, without any input from the more moderate members of Pierce's administration. At the behest of Salmon P. Chase, now a free-soil Democratic senator from Ohio, Douglas agreed to postpone for a week debate on the bill. Chase, Joshua Giddings, a free-soil Whig congressman from Ohio, Charles Sumner, newly elected free-soil senator from Massachusetts, and Gerrit Smith, an abolitionist congressman from New York, drafted a harsh indictment of Douglas and his Kansas-Nebraska Bill. Entitled "Appeal to the Independent Democrats," the document created an immediate sensation when it appeared in Washington, D.C.'s antislavery journal, the *National Era*, on January 24, 1854. The "Appeal" declared that the repeal of the Missouri Compromise was wrong and that it was wicked and morally bankrupt. Douglas was accused of sinful motives by condoning slavery in what had been free territory for the sordid end of purchasing support for his presidential ambitions. Chase and his coadjutors followed up the attack on Douglas and the Kansas-Nebraska bill by tacking on an amendment to the proposed legislation that gave the people of a territory the power to exclude slavery. Lewis Cass, speaking for the administration Democrats, indicated that the majority in the Senate would accept Chase's amendment if he would also add a provision that would give the people of a territory the power also to introduce slavery. When Chase refused, his amendment was voted down. What had begun as proposed legislation for strengthening the Democratic party had now produced the opposite effect, creating a situation similar to the moral, economic, and sectional controversy that very nearly broke up the Union in 1850.

Public opinion, presumably quiescent since the Compromise agreement, had in reality been slowly moving toward opposite poles. The publication of Harriet Beecher Stowe's novel about slavery, *Uncle Tom's Cabin*, which became a best seller in the United States and abroad, had helped bring about a change in public opinion. Northerners who read the book tended to view slavery as an outrage against humanity. Southerners who took exception to Stowe's vivid and compelling indictment of slavery were impelled to defend the institution, which they insisted had been misrepresented in the interest of melodrama. This explosion of emotion, combined with further deterioration of the Whig party and the rise of nativism in response to the wave of European immigration, were eroding political landmarks, moving the public towards extreme solutions offered by aspiring politicians.

It was in this disruptive context that the Kansas-Nebraska bill and "The Appeal to the Independent Democrats" worked their mischief. Once committed, Douglas could not turn back. Utilizing all his powers of argument, his prestige, and his mastery of parliamentary tactics, he forced the bill through Congress by the narrowest of margins. It received President Pierce's signature on May 29, 1854. Legislatures in ten northern states had either condemned the proposed legislation or passed resolutions that denied the propriety of the bill. Only in Illinois, where Douglas partisans controlled the legislature, was there a vote of approval, but opinion in the state was sharply divided.

Douglas left Washington soon after the adjournment of Congress in early August 1854. Along the route, the senator got a taste of the political uproar his Kansas-Nebraska Act had touched off in the North. "I could travel from Boston to Chicago," he remarked, "by the light of my own effigy. All along the Western Reserve of Ohio, I could find my effigy on every tree we passed." Douglas could discount the Western Reserve as abolitionist country, the home territory of such violent antislavery persons as Joshua Giddings and Edward Wade, who had helped draft Chase's "Appeal to the Independent Democrats." But he was dismayed and his confidence shaken by the hostility shown him when he sought to explain his position to a huge crowd that assembled before the balcony of his hotel in Chicago. He was constantly interrupted with groans and hisses. Responding to the temper of the crowd, he put aside his manuscript and challenged his critics. But this gesture was to no avail, and the pugnacious little senator became infuriated. He finally lost his temper to the great amusement of the crowd, and jamming his stovepipe hat on his head declared, "It is now Sunday morning; I'll go to church and you can go to hell."

In the South only two of the legislatures then in session approved of the bill. Others adjourned without taking any action. Whigs in the northern states were almost as vehemently opposed, while northern Democrats were sharply divided. The situation was ripe for the creation of a new party system based on a sectional alignment, with slavery in the territories as the overriding issue. Apprehension about southern intentions was again widespread in the North. And events in the summer of 1854 if anything increased tensions. A rash of filibustering expeditions that apparently attempted to extend slave territory southward at the expense of Spain and Central American republics followed closely after the passage of the Kansas-Nebraska bill. Although the timing of these expeditions was coincidental, it was widely believed in the North that the Act was part of a southern conspiracy to extend slavery nationwide. Another controversy arose when southern Democrats hailed the Pierce administration's forceful diplomacy with Spain over the seizure by Cuban authorities of an American vessel, the *Black Warrior*. Many northern papers on the other hand saw in the *Black Warrior* affair proof of the administration's intention to seize the island. Fears of southern aggression were further intensified when American ministers to three leading European nations met at Ostend, Belgium, and issued a provocative statement that demanded that Spain sell Cuba to the United States or risk the consequences, which they implied would be seizure by force. The ministers, James M. Mason of Virginia, Pierre Soulé of Louisiana, and James Buchanan of Pennsylvania, were leading Democrats and all defenders of or apologists for slavery. Their statement, which became known as the Ostend Manifesto, was widely publicized in the European and the American press. It was considered to be administration policy until Secretary of State William L. Marcy disavowed it in the summer of 1854 and made public the diplomatic correspondence with Spain over Cuba in the spring of the following year.

Birth of the Republican Party

By then steps had been taken to form a new party on the issue of slavery in the territories. Anti-Nebraska Whigs and Democrats in several northern and western states had formed state organizations. In the fall of 1854, Abraham Lincoln made a series of speeches in Illinois where he attacked the Kansas-Nebraska Act and its author, Douglas. Lincoln had several objects in mind. He wanted to fix in the public mind as much as possible the threat the act posed to free institutions everywhere. He wanted to demonstrate that slavery itself was immoral and that the Founding Fathers believed it to be so. But as a law-abiding citizen he respected constitutional guarantees for its protection in the states where it existed, not in the territories. Finally Lincoln wanted desperately to be elected to the United States Senate. He had achieved leadership of the Whig party in Illinois just as it was breaking up as a national institution. With anti-Nebraska feeling running strong in his state, however, Lincoln hoped to capitalize on it and bring his Whig organization behind him. His goal was the Senate seat of James Shields, a Douglas Democrat, which was up for election. (Eventually, however, the Illinois legislature would select Lyman Trumbull, an anti-Nebraska Democrat.)

In what amounted to a free-swinging debate, Lincoln went after Douglas who replied with as much vigor, if not more. In fact at Peoria on October 16, 1854, Douglas forced Lincoln to admit that while he opposed slavery he did not believe in social or political equality for blacks. Lincoln failed in his campaign for the United States Senate. His speeches and impromptu replies to Douglas, however, marked him as a powerful and persuasive free-soil Whig and as the most articulate orator of anti-Nebraska politicians in Illinois. But Illinois lagged in putting together a political coalition that was opposed to slavery in the territories. In neighboring states, a new party based on this principle had already come into being while Lincoln was seeking election to the United States Senate as an anti-Nebraska Whig.

Leading Whigs and Democrats had formed a national organization which met at a preliminary convention in Pittsburgh in the early spring of 1856. The leadership consisted of Salmon P. Chase of Ohio; the Jacksonian Democrat Francis P. Blair and his sons Montgomery and Francis Jr., representing the border states of Maryland and Missouri; Gideon Welles, the astute newspaper editor from Connecticut and his associate from that state, former free-soil Democratic senator John M. Niles; Preston King, William H. Seward, and Thurlow Weed from New York; and from Massachusetts, Charles Francis Adams and Charles Summer. The new party was in reality a coalition of politicians united only on the issue of slavery in the territories. As such it encountered serious conflict that for a time threatened to divert it from its goal and weaken its organization.

For the past two years the nativist movement and its political arm, the American party (or Know-Nothing party, as it was popularly called), had cast off its purely local character and its secrecy to emerge as a cohesive entity in the important states of Massachusetts, Connecticut, New York, Pennsylvania, and Ohio. The party's intolerant, nativist appeal had also made considerable headway in the border slave states and even in the Deep South. Former Whig politicans who were finding no future in their party structure had embraced the Know-Nothing cause. But the Know Nothings were not exclusively ex-Whigs. Nor was this party, which soon abandoned its derisive nickname for the broader appeal of the name American party, solely dedicated to nativism. Nathaniel P. Banks, for example, a leading Massachusetts Democrat, opposed the Kansas-Nebraska Act but joined the American party because it promised more immediate political advantage in the Bay State. If there were antislavery members within the American party, there were also those from the slave states who were staunch defenders of the institution. There were also those from all sections who sought to divert the public mind from the slavery issue by building on popular fears of alien subversion of traditional morals and values.

For a time it was questionable whether the Republican antislavery coalition could survive the nativist threat now so earnestly propagated. Republican strategists, however, managed to hold their party together. They emphasized democratic themes such as opportunity for immigrants that had always claimed a high place in public opinion. In espousing such an immigration policy, the Republicans separated the Roman Catholic element, which they condemned as un-American, from the Protestant element, mainly German and British recent immigrants, which they supported. Thus they could capitalize on widespread anti-Catholic feeling in the North and the Midwest, yet still approve a liberal immigration policy. Salmon P. Chase won election as the first Republican governor of the important state of Ohio in part by relying on these tactics. Fusion was not so successful in other northern states; a beginning had been made, however. After the elections in November 1854, the Republican party gained further momentum as the Pierce administration's policy in Kansas faltered and popular sovereignty came to be seen as unworkable.

Bleeding Kansas

While the Kansas-Nebraska bill was being debated in Congress, an abolitionist and gifted promoter, Eli Thayer, incorporated the Massachusetts Emigrant Aid Society to people the new territory with free soilers. His project gained almost instant popularity in the Northeast when Horace Greeley's influential *New York Tribune* and William Cullen Bryant's *Evening Post* gave the society extensive favorable publicity. Many monied northerners subscribed to its stock, and Thayer went on an extensive tour that raised considerable sums. More important than these promotion efforts, Thayer tapped a strain of moral fervor that existed among the educated and the articulate throughout the North. Free soil in the Kansas territory soon became a popular issue. The success of Thayer's campaign also inspired a vigorous reaction from proslavery elements, especially in Missouri, whose slave population was located primarily in those counties just across the Missouri River from Kansas. There was also a southern emigrant aid society incorporated in Charleston, South Carolina, to promote settlement in the territory. In the last analysis neither company was a financial success, nor did they populate the territory. Only about 1,200 free state emigrants settled in Kansas under the auspices of Thayer's company. The publicity Thayer inspired, however, resulted in a land rush which quickly took on speculative proportions.

David R. Atchison, a Democratic senator from Missouri and a strident defender of slavery who was one of the contingent that had persuaded Douglas to include an explicit repeal of the Missouri Compromise in his Nebraska bill, was a leader in creating proslavery sentiment in the territory. Slavery in Missouri was already in precarious condition. Slave owners were abandoning the state for the rich cotton lands of east Texas. Atchison felt that this process could be halted if Kansas were eventually to become a slave state. A reckless politician, he was quite willing to destroy the principle of popular sovereignty if it served his ends. Thus early on he led a band of Missourians to the territory. Their main purpose was to cast a vote for a government that protected slavery.

In the fall of 1854 President Pierce appointed a full slate of territorial officials for Kansas, which was attracting far more immigrants than Nebraska to the north. For governor he chose a Democratic party hack from Pennsylvania, Andrew H. Reeder. Samuel D. Lecompte, a slavery advocate, was appointed chief justice. But other members of the territorial government provided an even representation of free-soil and slavery interests. All were Democratic party regulars devoted to carrying out the administration policy. Reeder arrived in the new territory on October 7. He construed administration policy to be popular sovereignty and to that end he ordered a census to be taken that would reveal, he hoped, the number of eligible voters.

The permanence of these residents was questionable, however, since the Kansas-Nebraska Act provided for no such requirement. Even so, former Missouri citizens constituted a majority of the early settlers because of their nearness to the territory. Most of these new arrivals were susceptible to the propaganda of Atchison and his proslavery zealots. Well aware of their immediate advantage, the Missourians sought to have Reeder organize the territory and hold elections for a legislature that would prepare a proslavery constitution. Reeder, however, rejected their contentions and ordered an election for a congressional delegate only. On election day well over 1,500 Missourians crossed the Missouri River and voted for one of Atchison's aides as delegate. There had been no need for such extralegal action because proslavery elements at the time enjoyed a comfortable advantage. Yet so indoctrinated were Atchison's followers that they would leave nothing to chance, however remote. The Missourians carried the election by an overwhelming margin, but less than half of the votes were legal.

Meanwhile Reeder moved ahead with the census, which was concluded in the early winter of 1855. It disclosed that the territory had a population of 8,500, of whom 242 were slaves. The governor then ordered an election for a legislature to be held on March 30. Again as in the election for a territorial delegate, Missourians moved in just long enough to cast a vote. Almost 5,500 votes were given for proslavery candidates, a mere 791 for free soil. Only about 25 percent of the votes cast were deemed legal, however. Though Reeder certified the elections in two-thirds of the voting districts, he had grave doubts about their validity, doubts that were confirmed by direct evidence of fraud that was presented to him during the weeks following the election.

So dismayed was Reeder at the results that he left Kansas for Washington to alert the administration about the situation in the territory. En route he made a series of public statements that accused Missourians of making a mockery of popular sovereignty. His comments were broadcast widely in the northern press. President Pierce had several meetings with his embattled governor, but yielding to southern pressure in his cabinet and in Congress he took no action.

On Reeder's return to Kansas, the proslavery legislature convened. Meeting at Shawnee Mission, only a few miles from the Missouri border, it proceeded to convert Kansas into a slave territory by brazenly overriding the governor's veto and passing laws that were in patent violation of the Bill of Rights. Reeder had been a force for impartial administration and executive action in the territory. Unfortunately he tarnished his image by becoming involved in some flagrant land speculations. Publicity generated by these deals coincided with a mounting campaign for his recall by the Shawnee Mission legislature and the militant proslavery bloc in Washington.

In the late summer of 1855, Pierce replaced Reeder with Wilson Shannon, an Ohio Democrat and an administration stalwart. By now free-soil settlers had arrived in much greater numbers, primarily from the Northwest and the antislavery regions of the border states, not from New England and Thayer's much advertised Emigrant Aid Company. They formed a distinct majority over proslavery elements. Like their rivals at Shawnee Mission, they too formed a political party at Big Springs, a hamlet near the major free-soil settlement of Lawrence. Styling the meeting as a "Free State Convention," they elected Reeder to be the Kansas congressional delegate, denounced the Shawnee Mission legislature as fraudulent, insisted on a new election, and sent out a call for a constitutional convention to be held at another free-soil hamlet, Topeka, twenty-five miles northwest of Lawrence.

Meeting on October 23 and November 11, thirty-four free-soil delegates approved a constitution that prohibited slavery, nominated a slate of "state" officers, and provided for an election of a legislature in opposition to the Shawnee Mission legislature. Charles Robinson, a moderate antislavery man, was designated governor over the more radical political adventurer James "Jim" Lane. The Topeka constitution was approved at a special election on December 15 by a lopsided but generally fair vote of 1,731 to 46. It was forwarded to Washington for action. At the same time, the free soilers approved of an election for state officers to be held on January 5, 1856.

Both sides were now moving towards an armed confrontation. But Governor Shannon, supported by ex-senator Atchison, who had finally realized that conflict would not serve his ends, interposed and brought the bloodless so-called "Wakarusa War" to an end. All of these proceedings were fully publicized in the national press, which focused attention on Kansas.

The halls of Congress reverberated with angry debate that became more sharply accented when the new Thirty-fourth Congress convened on December 3, 1855. For the first time, members of the recently formed Republican party, adamantly opposed to slavery in the territories and frankly sectional in their agenda and their appeal, were ready to do parliamentary battle against popular sovereignty, or "southern rights," and those Democrats and Know-Nothings who would support slavery in Kansas. To them slavery was a local practice, but freedom was national. Northerners like Douglas who denied the power of Congress to prescribe the social institutions of the territories or those who followed President Pierce in his policy of coexistence with slavery in Kansas were denounced as "doughfaces." Republicans had recently attacked the Kansas-Nebraska Act for repealing the Missouri Compromise. Now for opposite reasons they lined themselves up with the proslavery extremists in opposing any reenactment of a geographic line between free and slave territory. Congress must act, they declared, but it must act for the cause of freedom everywhere. They pointed to the example of Kansas when they pronounced popular sovereignty as a political snare and delusion.

The Republicans were captained by resourceful leaders. Henry Wilson, the rough-featured, rough-spoken shoemaker from Massachusetts turned free-soil politician, ably seconded the cultivated but tactless moral reformer Charles Sumner. William H. Seward from New York, suave wirepuller and congressional logroller with deepseated antislavery convictions, complemented the tough, profane senator from Ohio, Benjamin Wade. A humorous, quick-witted veteran of the free-soil movement, John P. Hale of New Hampshire, added his talents to the antislavery phalanx.

Public attention in Washington at the end of November 1855 was riveted not on the Senate but on the House where a monumental struggle was in process. At stake was the Speakership. According to House rules an absolute majority was necessary for election. Although the Republicans as a party bloc had the most members, Democrats and Know Nothings together constituted a majority of sixteen votes. For ballot after ballot, the two coalitions held firm to their candidates. It was not until February 1856 that enough Know Nothings voted with the Republicans to change the majority rule to a plurality and then only because Republican leaders were willing to support former Democrat and Know Nothing Nathaniel P. Banks of Massachusetts. He was elected Speaker by 103 votes to 100 for William Aiken of South Carolina, a moderate Democrat. The Banks election foreshadowed a fusion between the Know Nothings and the Republicans. The latter party was slowly gaining an ascendancy with its broader appeal that gave the antislavery movement a much wider popular base.

While the House was in the throes of organizational turmoil, the Senate had already begun debate on Kansas. President Pierce in his annual message had denounced the Topeka "free state" constitution. Brushing aside the complaints of ex-Governor Reeder and the evidence of fraud in the first territorial election, Pierce supported the Shawnee Mission legislature. He declared that this body should take immediate steps to hold a constitutional convention as a precondition for admission of Kansas as a slave state.

Though troubled by improprieties in the election of the Shawnee Mission government, Douglas backed the President. He embodied his views in a majority report from his Committee on Territories that declared the Shawnee Mission legislature to be the only legal government in Kansas. Douglas blamed the confusion in Kansas on outside interference. Sumner and Seward attacked Douglas's propositions with such effectiveness that they forced the Illinois senator to admit fraud had been practiced in the territorial election. Seward offered his own bill that would admit Kansas under the free-soil Topeka constitution. Like that of the Shawnee Mission government, this document too was biased and not an appropriate referendum on the slavery issue. The United States Senate confirmed Shannon as governor of the territory by a close vote, but Douglas was unable to gain approval for the Shawnee Mission government in his bill.

Events in Kansas continued to dramatize the conflict in Congress. A proslavery mob descended on Lawrence, burned "Governor" Robinson's house and the Free State Hotel, sacked the office of the only newspaper in town, *The Herald of Freedom*, and destroyed its press. The mob then went on to several private dwellings which were looted. One person was accidentally killed before the mob dispersed and left town. The raid was exaggerated in the northern metropolitan dailies and their country editions. Readers were led to believe that Lawrence had been completely destroyed and that many innocent people had been killed by "border ruffians." The incident was, of course, not a creditable one, but the distortion raised public emotions far beyond appropriate levels.

Nor did the murderous activities of John Brown, a fanatical antislavery man who combined a puritan sense of mission with a distorted Old Testament sense of vengeance, ease the troubled situation. Shortly after the attack on Lawrence, Brown with a small band of armed men stole into some rude dwellings on the banks of the Pottawatomie Creek at night. There they seized five unarmed, helpless settlers who had crossed over from Missouri and murdered them in cold blood.

Responsible persons in the territory, whether they supported slavery or not, were horrified at this act of wanton violence. Neither Brown nor any member of his group was ever brought to justice for this particular crime. Even ardent free soilers were troubled at Brown's foray and saw in it a symptom of the utter lawlessness that stalked Kansas. Two years after the event, John Sherman, then a congressman from Ohio and a Republican stalwart, met Brown in Chicago. Sherman asked the stoop-shouldered, graybearded Yankee about the Pottawatomie affair. As Sherman recalled, Brown replied with spirit that the settlers had not been murdered but had been arrested, tried by jury, convicted, and executed. "The arrest, trial and execution," commented Sherman drily on the affair, "must have been done during one night."

Brown's bloody escapade had been preceded by a vicious attack on Charles Sumner as he was sitting at his desk in the Senate chamber. Two days earlier Sumner had delivered a diatribe in very bad taste against the elderly senator from South Carolina, Andrew Butler, and against Douglas. His gross rhetorical display, replete with offensively sexual and scatological metaphors, shocked most of his colleagues irrespective of party. If Preston Brooks, an emotionally unstable congressman from South Carolina, had not decided to beat brutally the Massachusetts senator as he sat defenseless in his chair, the repugnant speech would have tarnished a good deal of Sumner's political luster among the educated and the articulate in the North. As it was, however, Sumner became an instant martyr, for he had been badly injured. It would be several years before he could return to the Senate. His empty chair and desk were visible reminders to northern visitors of what they chose to believe was another victim in the long battle for freedom.

Southerners on the other hand who had been exposed to Sumner's intemperate, indeed frequently crude, reflections on their character (which were quoted out of context or exaggerated in their newspapers) regarded the assault as just deserts for an unprincipled display of northern aggression. Senators

Davis and Slidell on the one hand, and senators Seward and Sumner on the other, now personified the progressive polarization along sectional lines of public opinion on the slavery issue.

CHAPTER FOUR

Disruption

In an atmosphere of mutual suspicion and uncertainty, the Know Nothings divided on the slavery issue. The proslavery faction, also known as the South Americans, nominated ex-president Millard Fillmore for president and Andrew J. Donelson of Tennessee, Andrew Jackson's nephew, for Vice President. At a subsequent convention the free-soil group, or North Americans, nominated Nathaniel P. Banks, current Speaker of the House, for President and William P. Johnston, a former Pennsylvania Whig, for Vice President. The new Republican party had already held a preliminary organizational convention in Pittsburgh. It was profiting from the split among the Know Nothings and a decline in nativist sentiment in the North and the Midwest as these regions began to share in an upsurge of world trade that followed the end of the Crimean War.

The Election of 1856

At their first nominating convention in Philadelphia, the Republicans brushed aside the claims of their antislavery veterans, Salmon P. Chase and William H. Seward, to nominate John C. Frémont, a popular figure who had gained recognition through his explorations of the Far West. The Republican platform came out boldly for the exclusion of slavery from the territories and for the admission of Kansas as a free state. In a concession to conservatives and moderates, however, the platform made no specific recommendation on slavery in the District of Columbia. Its wording on the nativist issue was also conciliatory to the North Americans while it called for liberty of conscience and equality for all American citizens. Emphasizing the coalition nature of the new party, the platform avoided any mention of tariff, currency, or banking, but it did endorse internal improvements of a "national character" at federal expense. And it expressly favored federal support for a transcontinental railroad.

After the convention Republican managers entered into a series of delicate negotiations with the North Americans and succeeded in having them drop their national presidential ticket. The North Americans accepted Frémont and the Republican nominee for Vice President, William Dayton, a former Whig from New Jersey. The American party now ceased to be a national political organization. A remnant of the party, primarily made up of South Americans, continued to support Fillmore for President. His candidacy attracted little attention though he would poll more than one-fifth of the votes in the November election.

The Democrats met in Cincinnati on June 2, 1856. The major candidates were Pierce, Buchanan, Cass, and Douglas. But the contest soon became a struggle between Buchanan and Douglas. Southern delegates generally supported the "Little Giant," but northerners even in former Douglas strongholds of the Midwest were not united in his behalf. When it became apparent that the convention was deadlocked, Douglas acting through a delegate from Kentucky took himself out of convention. Buchanan was nominated on the seventeenth ballot. John C. Breckinridge of Kentucky, a staunch Douglas supporter, received the vice presidential nomination.

Few candidates for President were as experienced in public office as Buchanan. But few public men to that time had such a background of political deviousness than this wrynecked wirepuller from Pennsylvania. His political escapades dated back to 1825, when as a congressman he engineered the "corrupt bargain" charge against John Quincy Adams and Henry Clay. After that he had been minister to Russia, a senator from Pennsylvania, secretary of state in the Polk administration and minister to Great Britain.

Predictably the Democratic platform supported the Kansas-Nebraska Act and included the standard party dogma on the tariff, internal improvements, banking, and the currency. The convention tabled a resolution that would have urged federal support for a highway to California. Nor did the platform mention a transcontinental railroad. In foreign policy it endorsed a vigorous assertion of the Monroe Doctrine in the Caribbean, but was silent on Cuba.

Although the Republican party was only a year old and was purely a coalition of formerly antagonistic groups held together by a single issue, the containment of slavery, its leadership managed to keep organizational problems to a minimum. Other than issuing some public letters carefully crafted by experienced political writers, Frémont made no pronouncement on policy that differed from his party's platform. Nor did Buchanan for that matter. Yet the campaign was a spirited one in which the margin of victory for the Democrats was narrow indeed. Buchanan received only a plurality of the votes cast; the American ticket garnered over 21 percent of the popular vote (872,000 out of 4,045,000) and won eight electoral votes. Obviously threats of secession from southern states if Frémont were elected had frightened a considerable number of conservative northern voters. The Republicans won eleven of the sixteen free states, while in the five that went Democratic, Frémont lost by scant margins. Buchanan won the election because his electoral vote majority in the South was greater than Frémont's was in the North. If political organizations were the great agents of national unity that they were claimed to be, the election of 1856 must be recorded as the end of an era. From now on sectional loyalties rather than party ties would determine the fate of the Union.

Dred Scott

The incoming Buchanan administration, recognizing the danger of disunion foretold by Kansas and by the emergence of the Republican party, sought immediately to reconcile differences over slavery in the territories. The Supreme Court had under review the appeal of Dred Scott, a slave who had been taken to Illinois, a free state, where he lived for two years and then to Fort Snelling, in what is now Minnesota, a free territory by virtue of the Missouri Compromise, where he also resided for several years. Scott was then returned to his native state of Missouri.

In 1846 a suit was brought in the Missouri courts alleging that Scott's residence in a free state and a free territory made him a free man. At first a jury trial declared Scott free under Missouri law. But on appeal to the state supreme court, the decision was reversed. The court held that the laws of a free state and territory did not affect Scott's status upon his return to Missouri. Scott's attorneys then began a new case in the federal circuit court for Missouri. They argued that Scott's residence in free territory made him not only a free man but a citizen of Missouri and thus entitled to sue his new alleged owner, John Sanford of New York, in federal court for his freedom. The circuit court accepted jurisdiction in the case, but then ruled that Missouri law governed Scott's status and hence he was still a slave. This decision prompted Scott's lawyers to appeal to the United States Supreme Court on a writ of error.

While Scott's various suits and appeals were being made,

the Compromise of 1850 and the Kansas-Nebraska Act of 1854 had made the question of slavery in the territories a prime political issue. Eminent lawyers were attracted to the case pending, Reverdy Johnson, formerly a senator from Maryland and Attorney General of the United States, considered to be one of the leading constitutional experts in the nation, headed counsel for Sanford, who was now technically Scott's owner. Henry S. Geyer, at that time a United States senator from Missouri, was Johnson's associate. Representing Scott was Montgomery Blair, elder son of Francis Preston Blair and one of the leading figures in the new Republican party.

The Supreme Court faced several questions. If it decided to rule on the case, it had first to address itself to the question of whether Scott was a citizen of Missouri and thus entitled to sue under the federal court's diversity-of-citizenship jurisdiction. If he were not a Missouri citizen, he could not bring suit against a citizen of another state. Yet the circuit court had permitted him to sue, and Sanford, his putative owner and the defendant in the case, had "pleaded over" once the court had accepted jurisdiction. So Scott's attorneys could argue that the jurisdictional question was closed. A second question involved Scott's residence in free territory. Did it make him permanently a free man? This issue tested Congress's power to prohibit slavery in any region and thus the constitutionality of the Missouri Compromise. But the court could also dodge this explosive issue simply by holding that the state courts had already determined the status of a resident black slave. For the past seven years, Congress had done the same thing by refusing to define precisely where slavery ended and freedom began.

At first a majority of the justices were inclined to avoid a controversial and essentially political interpretation. But then the five justices from the slave states, headed by Chief Justice Roger B. Taney, all of whom thought the Missouri Compromise was unconstitutional, changed their minds. Perhaps the opinions of the two northern justices, John McLean and Benjamin R. Curtis, who felt just as adamantly that the

Compromise was constitutional, pushed the majority to attempt a settlement of the territorial issue, but this is far from clear. More likely, the southern justices themselves saw an opening to have the court utilize its favorable image and its high prestige to resolve a national controversy that had taken on a dangerous coloration.

President-elect Buchanan had also entered the picture by corresponding with both Justice John Catron of Tennessee and Justice Robert C. Grier, a fellow Pennsylvanian. Buchanan urged the court to rule on the case in such a way that the agitation on slavery would be lessened, which in turn, he thought, would ease the dangers that beset the Union. In the end all of the justices wrote opinions. There were slight differences among the majority justices on certain points and on the line of argument taken. But the justices themselves considered the Chief Justice's argument to be the opinion of the court. The two northern justices, McLean and Curtis, filed dissents.

On March 6, 1857, two days after Buchanan's inauguration, the Court rendered its fateful decision. The substance of Taney's opinion was contained in the following points:

1) Blacks could not qualify as citizens of the United States because they had not held citizenship at the time the Constitution was adopted; they had then been regarded as racially inferior. Nor could the subsequent action of any state confer national citizenship.

2) As a result, blacks could not sue in federal courts under the Constitution's diversity-of-citizenship clause. Hence the federal circuit court in Missouri had erred in taking jurisdiction of Scott's case.

3) The Missouri Compromise did not make Scott free. It was unconstitutional because it exceeded the delegated powers of Congress and deprived a citizen of his property (slave property) without due process of law as provided by the Fifth Amendment to the Constitution.

4) Nor was Scott free by virtue of his stay in Illinois, for once he returned to Missouri, that state's law governed him.

5) So Scott was still a slave, not a citizen, and not qualified to sue in federal court.

Curtis's and McLean's dissenting opinions argued persuasively that Congress had the power under Section II of Article IV of the Constitution to make "all needful rules and regulations respecting the territory or other property belonging to the United States" and that this clause included the power to allow or prohibit slavery. The Missouri Compromise was therefore constitutional. Curtis also pointed out that historically free blacks had been citizens of the states. In 1787 five states had granted citizenship to blacks. Indeed in many of the free states they were currently citizens. With respect to the power of Congress to legislate on slavery in the territories, Curtis detailed numerous instances where it had acted either to uphold or restrain the institution. He made one of his more telling points on the matter of the Fifth Amendment, contending that the due process clause, a descendent of the Magna Carta, could not serve as a mainstay of slavery. In addition, referring to Taney's point that blacks were not citizens of the United States and therefore could not sue in federal courts, he explained that the citizenship question was not a legitimate one for the court to address owing to the technical status of Sanford's appeal. According to Curtis, Taney's argument and those of the six other justices who concurred with him was not only faulty but lacked any sense of reality.

Not since the decision in *Marbury v. Madison* in 1803 had the court exercised judicial review over an act of Congress, although the Kansas-Nebraska Act had repealed de facto the Missouri Compromise three years earlier (except where it extended to the Minnesota Territory). Yet when the court took this grave step, it was declaring unconstitutional the ideological and political foundations of the Republican party. Very nearly half of the electorate had just voted to support the principles now outlawed. At the same time the decision dealt a heavy blow to Douglas's moderate position of popular sovereignty. If Congress could not directly legislate against slavery, argued Taney, it could not authorize a territorial legislature to do so. This position called into question whether the people in a territory had any say about the status of slavery. The Court went still further when it gave constitutional protection to slaves as property. Was not the federal government then bound to protect property in the territories regardless of the will of the inhabitants? Taney seemed to come close to calling for a federal slave code.

Such an affront to public opinion in the free states could not be tolerated without risking intense public outrage. The *New York Tribune*, for example, reiterated Salmon P. Chase's succinct phrase summing up what most of its readers felt about the decision. "Slavery is national, freedom is local," it said. The decision that the Buchanan administration had hoped would calm agitation and remove a divisive element from politics had had just the reverse effect. No sooner had the ruling been disseminated throughout the nation than Republican politicians and opinion makers began suggesting a conspiracy on the part of the Buchanan administration to expand the institution of slavery. Abraham Lincoln, an aspiring Republican politician in Illinois, charged that the decision proved a prior arrangement between Douglas, Taney, and Buchanan. Later Douglas demonstrated that the charge was wholly without foundation as far as he was concerned.

Even though the Taney decision dealt only with slavery in the territories, might not the next step be to extend federal protection of the institution in the free states, thus converting the United States into a totally slave-holding republic? Republican newspapers and orators asked this question, fixing on Taney's sentence, "The right of property in a slave is distinctly and expressly affirmed in the constitution." That there was little evidence for raising such an inquiry made no difference to those who fed on public alarm. Interestingly, however, the New York case of *Lemmon v. People*, involving that state's denial to slaveowners of the right of transit with their slaves, *might* have led to a even stricter exposition of the principles laid down in the Dred Scott decision. This test of a state's right to exclude slavery was never heard, for the Civil War and postwar constitutional amendments made the issue a moot one. In the last analysis the Dred Scott case widened the gulf between the sections, further encouraging mutual fears.

Kansas, Second Phase

With the Dred Scott decision casting a deep shadow over the opening weeks of the Buchanan administration, the new President sought to deal with the festering Kansas problem that had baffled politicians and distracted the country for the past three years. Prior to this time, Wilson Shannon, Pierce's second governor, had been replaced because like Reeder he had tried to be impartial and because he had used federal troops rather than the local militia to restore order. In applying this kind of force, even though he acted within his instructions, Shannon brought a storm of criticism on the administration. Pierce accepted Shannon's resignation. He sent yet a third governor to the distracted territory, John W. Geary. Six feet five inches tall, Geary was a fine figure of a man. A native of Pennsylvania, a lawyer, and a veteran of the Mexican War, he had served as mayor of San Francisco and was prominent in Democratic politics. With a wealth of administrative experience behind him, Geary combined a talent for leadership with some political skill. Almost at once he was called upon to draw on all of those qualities. He had no sooner taken over the government when Atchison, at the head of a proslavery force of some 2,500 men, invaded the territory in retaliation for a foray by free state men that for a time menaced the village of Lecompton, a temporary center of proslavery activity. Geary managed to halt Atchison's force without bloodshed, after which it returned to Missouri.

For a time Geary had bandaged the "Bleeding Kansas" portrayed in the northern press, but only for a time. There was too much at stake in this territory, the leading edge of conflict between the two sections. Buchanan, though susceptible to southern influence, and who had a majority of southerners in his cabinet, was determined to give popular sovereignty a fair trial in Kansas. Although the Dred Scott decision had weakened the legality of the concept, the President went ahead with his plans.

As Geary's replacement he chose Robert J. Walker, a Pennsylvanian who had moved south and had served as a senator from Mississippi. Walker had gained additional national prominence when, as Polk's secretary of the treasury, he designed the tariff that became known as the Walker Tariff. If any Democratic politician could solve the Kansas puzzle, Walker, a shrewd politician and a hardheaded realist, seemed the most likely candidate. Prudently he worked out with Buchanan what he thought would be the specifics of a settlement before he agreed to take on the assignment. In a public letter that was given wide publicity, he expressed his belief in popular sovereignty and his insistence that only actual residents of the territory "by a fair and regular vote, unaffected by fraud or violence, must be permitted in adopting their State Constitution to decide for themselves what shall be their social institutions." He concluded his statement by declaring that the Buchanan administration supported his position. Walker also cleared his policy with Douglas in Chicago before going further west.

Despite his careful planning Walker was unable to prevail on the free soilers, who were now a decided majority but who refused to vote for delegates to a constitutional convention that the proslavery legislature had ordered. The free soilers contended that the legislature had been elected fraudulently. All of this was of course true, but in taking such a legalistic stand, the free state faction was refusing to assess the situation in practical terms. If they had accepted Walker's plea, they would have elected a majority of free soil delegates, who then would have drafted a free-soil constitution. In boycotting the election they handed the initiative to the proslavery minority. Walker also lost support from southerners and all those who backed popular sovereignty because of his apparant partiality to the free-soil faction. He had not been in Kansas long when, over his objections, a constitution with a slavery clause was adopted at Lecompton. The Lecompton convention also provided for a referendum, but only on the slavery clause, not the constitution itself. The proposition was worded in such a way that whatever the vote, slavery would be upheld.

Before that convention met Walker had managed to have another election for the legislature. This time the free soilers went to the polls. Astonishingly, the proslavery element won narrowly, claiming 1628 votes from Oxford, a hamlet in unsettled Johnson County and 1200 votes from three voting places in another unsettled area, McGee County. When Walker discovered that these votes were bogus—1,601 names, for instance, came from Williams's *Cincinnati Directory*—he rejected them. The free soilers now had an overwhelming majority. Walker, however, had already resolved to leave Kansas. He had not been given the support he felt he needed to control the situation in the territory. He spoke with Douglas in Chicago and informed him fully of the travesty that proslavery elements had made of popular sovereignty. Walker met with Buchanan and his cabinet and argued against the Lecompton constitution, which he maintained did not represent the feelings of a majority of the Kansas settlers. But his arguments were of no avail. The administration was determined to support a bill conferring territorial status upon the Lecompton government. On December 3 an angry Douglas called on the President to demand an explanation. Buchanan's secretary of the navy, Isaac Toucey, was with the President at the time. A Democratic party regular from Connecticut, Toucey was one of those northern politicians who consistently favored the South on public questions. Although Douglas and Buchanan had been and still were political rivals and were scarcely on the best of personal terms, they were at first both civil with each other. Controlling his feelings, Douglas advised Buchanan not to recommend the new Kansas enabling bill, which supported the Lecompton constitution. Buchanan, whose message supporting the act had already been written, disagreed with all

Douglas had said. He declared that he would urge acceptance and make the new bill an administration measure. "If you do," said Douglas, his composure beginning to fray, "I will denounce it the moment your message is read." Buchanan too became irritated at the tone of Douglas's voice and the deep scowl that now creased his forehead. He moved to terminate the interview, but not before he theatened the senator with punitive action. "Mr. Douglas," the white-haired President said in measured tones, "I desire you to remember that no Democrat ever differed from an administration of his own choice without being crushed." Then he alluded to two senators, one from Virginia, the other from New York, who had opposed their administration's bank policies and were driven out of the party. "Beware the fate of Tallmadge and Rives," warned Buchanan. "Mr. President," replied a defiant and by now a thoroughly angry Douglas, "I wish you to remember that General Jackson is dead."

Toucey at this point sought to ease the tense situation that had developed between the two men. He pointed out that Douglas's position would produce a split in the Democratic party that could only benefit their political adversaries, the Republicans. Douglas concurred. "Why, my dear sir," said Toucey, "you agree with me in everything—I don't see how we can disagree at all." "Certainly not," said Douglas, as he was turning to leave. "We *can't* disagree, Mr. Toucey; it's impossible; for you are always right on a constitutional question, and while the Constitution declares that *Congress* may admit new States, it hasn't a word in it about *Cabinets* admitting them."

The President's message went to Congress the next day. Among other recommendations it urged Congress to adopt the organization of the Kansas territory under the Lecompton constitution. At this point Stephen A. Douglas parted with administration policy. He maintained vigorously that the Lecompton constitution scorned popular sovereignty. The President retaliated by removing Douglas supporters from their federal posts, and in effect reading them out of the Democratic party. He also relied on the bestowal of patronage and the threat of withholding it to bring congressmen into line.

While debate in Congress on the Kansas bill was raging, Henry S. Foote, the peppery senator from Mississippi, dropped in on Howell Cobb, the secretary of the treasury. Cobb asked Foote to do what he could to push the Kansas bill. Foote avoided any commitment by asking Cobb what he thought of its prospects for passage. The fat, cheerful Cobb said, "Oh, I think we will get it through, we have now secured almost as many votes as will be necessary to its passage; and you know that this Department is always, in such a struggle, good for at least twenty votes."

But Douglas was a tough and wiley adversary. In fact his belligerent course toward the Buchanan administration caused some Republican leaders who previously had been free-soil Democrats to urge his defection to their party. Gideon Welles, now a member of the Republican National Committee and a major figure in organizing the campaign of 1860, felt no compunction about addressing Douglas as "an old brother Democrat." In his letter to the "Little Giant" he said, "I have not a doubt there is to be a revolution. You must go forward in this work & lead the host to battle & to victory. It is your mission & the more trying the ordeal to you personally, the greater will be the reward." But Douglas refused this and other tentative advances and resolved to battle the President within the party and on his own terms.

A congressional deadlock on the Lecompton issue was finally resolved through a compromise measure offered by William H. English of Indiana. Under the English compromise, Congress would send the constitution back to Kansas, where the inhabitants of the territory would have an opportunity to accept or reject slavery. If they accepted the constitution, Kansas could become a state at once and receive a land grant. If they rejected the constitution, Kansas would remain a territory until a census indicated that it had 90,000 inhabitants, which according to the census of 1850 was the minimum population necessary for the election of one congressman. Any land grant, of course, would be determined by Congress at the time of admission. Kansas voters again went to the polls and in a fair referendum rejected the Lecompton constitution by a vote of 11,300 to 1,788. Kansas could not become a state until 1861.

Lincoln and Douglas

The Kansas problem and the split in the Democratic party between the Douglas forces and those of Buchanan focused attention on the senatorial race in Illinois. Douglas was a candidate for reelection. He was being challenged again by Abraham Lincoln, who had gained a significant following among Republicans of the Midwest. Forty-nine years old at the time, Lincoln was in the prime of his life, a highly successful corporation lawyer who combined courtroom skills with a well-developed political instinct. The epitome of the western self-made man, Lincoln sprang from the humblest beginnings and throughout his political and professional career radiated the practical, down-to-earth style much admired in the rural America of the mid-nineteenth century. But behind the simple, rough-hewn demeanor, Lincoln was a confirmed idealist and humanitarian. He had built on the political reputation that he established during his 1854 campaign for the United States Senate. His clear and logical articulation of current issues found favor with educated, urban audiences while his homely touch and sense of humor appealed to the country folk. He was also recognized as a shrewd politician whose position on the slavery issue was consistent yet moderate. In 1858 he was a leading figure in the Illinois Republican organization.

Lincoln had never disguised his hatred of slavery as a moral evil, but he had also repeatedly declared that he was a law-abiding person. Since the Constitution upheld the institution as a local concern, he would not disturb it where it existed under state protection and local custom. Yet drawing on the Declaration of Independence, Lincoln had often expressed the opinion that slavery was inconsistent with human rights and natural law. Like Chase and other free soilers, he followed the precedent of the Northwest Ordinance in maintaining that the territories be kept free of the taint of slavery, a popular stand in the midwestern free states. As early as 1847, Salmon P. Chase had argued before the United States Supreme Court in the Van Zandt case that "when a slave leaves the jurisdiction of a state he ceases to be a slave, because he continues to be a man and leaves behind him the law which made him a slave." Lincoln and many other politicians in the two major parties who were sympathetic to the free-soil position accepted Chase's dictum. Lincoln also derived his position on slavery from a liberal interpretation of the territorial clause in Article IV of the Constitution. He also accepted Chase's argument that cited the slavery clauses of the Constitution as precursors of freedom, thereby linking the Constitution to the Declaration. Noting that the framers had carefully avoided any specific mention of slavery and had abolished the international slave trade after 1808, Chase and Lincoln maintained that the original intent of the framers pointed towards eventual emancipation. Despite his consistent antislavery stand, Lincoln was judged to be more moderate on the slavery issue than Chase or Seward, the leading candidates for the Republican nomination in 1860.

Both Douglas and Lincoln conducted vigorous campaigns not just in Illinois but also in Ohio during 1858 and 1859. Lincoln said that he made 63 speeches while Douglas declared that he gave 130. Whatever the number, the two candidates tended to respond to each other's positions, which had narrowed to a discussion of slavery in the light of recent events.

In July 1858 Lincoln suggested that the two candidates meet face to face in formal debates, a proposition that Douglas, who was far better known even in Illinois, accepted reluctantly. Throughout the late summer, the two men met at seven towns: Ottawa, Freeport, Jonesboro, Charleston, Galesburg, Quincy, and Alton. What resulted was not only a thorough exposition of their conflicting views, but an intellectual discussion of slavery that went far deeper than the one-issue abolitionist argument and the professions of the politicians, whether defenders or opponents of slavery.

In the debates Lincoln forced Douglas to define popular sovereignty in the light of the recent Dred Scott decision. At Freeport he asked for clarification and got a response he knew he would get since Douglas had already explained his position on the issue. Douglas's prompt reply, which became known as the Freeport Doctrine, was that "slavery cannot exist a day or an hour anywhere unless it is supported by local police regulations." This statement placed him in the awkward role of accepting nominally the constitutional force of the Dred Scott decision, but at the same time demonstrating that it had no practical effect if it ran counter to public opinion at any given place or time. Once he had Douglas's answer on this point, Lincoln moved to other considerations of the moral and social injustice of slavery. At Alton, he made his point most eloquently when he cast the slavery question in the broadest possible terms. "It is," he said, "the eternal struggle between these two principles—right and wrong throughout the world." Douglas, however, stuck to a position that made sense in Illinois, a state whose southern half bordered on the slave states of Missouri and Kentucky. Privately Douglas was opposed to slavery, but not on moral grounds. He saw the institution in practical terms as an anachronism that could be set on the road to extinction through a kind of natural containment. Devoted to the concept of popular sovereignty, he was certain that slavery would not spread into territories where geography as well as public opinion inhibited it. Slavery to him posed no moral dilemma, but was simply an uneconomic, unnecessarily harsh subordination of one group of people to another.

Lincoln, too, was forced to meld the practical with the abstract. In doing so he again adhered to a position where the civil rights of blacks were carefully circumscribed. At the Ottawa debate, he repeated what he had said at Peoria in 1854 on the position of blacks in American society. He would not grant them Illinois citizenship. He was opposed to intermarriage between whites and blacks and he did not think them competent to serve on juries. Other than these specifics that Lincoln probably had to define for his audience, he accorded blacks all the natural rights described in the Declaration of Independence. As he phrased it, "and particularly the right to eat the bread, without leave of anybody else, which his own hand earns, he is my equal and the equal of Judge Douglas and of every living man."

From a modern viewpoint one can charge Lincoln with hypocrisy on civil rights during the debates. But he did try to reconcile his high moral purpose and his strongly felt anti-slavery beliefs with the problem of race adjustment which he foresaw and which he knew, considering the state of predominant white opinion at the time, had to be faced at some point. Lincoln after all was engaged in a political contest against a resourceful adversary. Within that context, he raised the level of the debate on slavery to a higher, more convincing level than had hitherto been achieved. Those paying close attention would have noted that he admitted the possibility of future black advancement and fulfillment of the promise of the Declaration.

Douglas won reelection to the United States Senate because of the way a previous Democratic majority had apportioned the state legislature. Even then Lincoln lost by only eight votes in the joint session. He actually gained a slight popular majority in the state. In spite of Douglas's reputation as a national figure and his political appeal within Illinois, Lincoln's performance in the debates, which were widely covered and well reported in the press, catapulted him to political prominence throughout the free states and within the leadership of the Republican party. It remained only for "the rail splitter," as Lincoln was now being nicknamed, to satisfy eastern leaders of the Republican party that he was sound on all matters of political concern. A personal appearance in the east was essential if he were to be considered for the Republican presidential nomination.

John Brown's Raid on Harpers Ferry

Republicans and Democrats were preparing for the elections of 1860 in a political atmosphere poisoned by the division in the Democratic party and the still festering wound of the Kansas controversy. Then a startling event brought the prospect of a sectional cleavage closer. In mid-October, just three weeks before the November elections, John Brown, the antislavery zealot who had left behind him a murderous trail in Kansas, headed a small armed band that captured the federal arsenal at Harpers Ferry, Virginia.

Brown was an impressive person. His implacable determination to eradicate slavery by force if necessary invested his personality with a sense of power that impressed many who listened to his discourses in New England and upstate New York. Abolitionists like Gerrit Smith, the rich New York landowner who favored direct action, supplied funds for Brown to purchase weapons and recruit volunteers. But they were unaware of Brown's specific plans. So certain was Brown of the righteousness of his cause and the support he thought he could expect from antislavery whites, free blacks, and the slaves themselves that he assumed a bold stroke would unleash a slave revolt throughout the South.

Accordingly he chose the arsenal at Harpers Ferry for his assault. The arsenal, which contained an abundance of arms and ammunition, was situated in a valley of the Blue Ridge Mountains where the borders of Virginia and Maryland meet. Many whites in the area were known to oppose slavery. Brown counted on some support from them. Early in the morning of October 16, 1859, Brown at the head of his small force of seventeen men, among whom were his own sons, overpowered the watchman, cut the telegraph lines, and seized the arsenal. He also took as hostages several prominent slave-owning citizens of the vicinity, and in doing so set off an alarm that alerted the community. Instead of the thousands of slaves that he expected would flock to Harpers Ferry, Brown was confronted with armed citizens and in short order a detachment of United States Marines under the command of Brevet Colonel Robert E. Lee. Brown retreated to the engine house, a substantial brick building, and for a time offered armed resistance. With most of his men dead and himself wounded, Brown's little garrison was overwhelmed by a direct assault. He was promptly taken to Richmond where he stood trial for treason, was found guilty, and was sentenced to be hanged.

The raid had failed utterly. No slave willingly joined Brown, but the southern press labeled it as an extreme and dangerous slave revolt. Brown's connection with northern abolitionists was scouted and hasty conclusions drawn that the "Black Republicans" of the North were determined to impose their will on the South through violent means if necessary. Rumors and hectic rhetoric continued to mount during Brown's trial. His Connecticut birth and his Mayflower ancestry, which he boasted of at his trial, was offered by stump speakers throughout the South as proof positive that all Yankees were potential enemies. Despite almost universal condemnation of the raid from leading citizens of northern society, including virtually all Republican politicians and public officials, the mood in the slave states remained suspicious, defensive, and downright hostile.

At the conclusion of his trial, Brown made the most of his opportunity to address the court. His five minute statement was most eloquent. In courting martyrdom, he made additional comments that were equally noble in character. And on the scaffold he comported himself with a dignity that some observers found sublime. His words did little or nothing to explain or ameliorate his actions in the slave states. But public opinion in the North, while still condemning his rash act, found the stuff of early Christian martyrs in John Brown. On the morning of his execution Brown gave his jailor a paper on which he had written his prophecy. "I John Brown," he said, "am now quite *certain* that the crimes of this *guilty land:* will never be purged away; but with Blood. I had, *as I now think:* vainly flattered myself that without *very much* bloodshed; it might be done." The conservative Republican lawyer George Templeton Strong, who had all along deprecated Brown's act, expressed a view shared by thoughtful persons in the North. "Old John Brown was hanged this morning; justly, say I, but his name may be a word of power for the next half century."

Over five years had elapsed since Stephen A. Douglas on that wintry afternoon in January 1854 took the fateful step and bowed to southern demands in framing the Kansas-Nebraska Act. It had been a period of rising tensions as the positions of the two sections on slavery became more sharply defined. The Kansas question had flamed up and for a time exacerbated regional differences. When that distracting issue finally ran its course, it left behind its own measure of smoldering resentment and mutual suspicions that the Dred Scott decision and Brown's assault on Harpers Ferry intensified.

Panic and Political Paralysis

While the political uproar over the decision was still at its height, the boom of the mid-fifties had come to an abrupt end in the industrializing North and Midwest. Panic in the money markets of London, Paris, and New York quickly led to the familiar suspension of specie payments and the frenzied dumping of securities on the market, mainly those of overcapitalized, overextended railroad companies. Financial collapse led to a sudden shortage of credit, widespread foreclosures on speculative properties, curtailment of manufacturing production, and consequent unemployment. Yet the Depression of 1857, which would last for the next five years, left the cotton-producing regions of the South relatively untouched. To some extent this economic anomaly was the result of tariff legislation that Congress approved at the behest of the Buchanan administration and its southern supporters. The Walker Tariff rates had been lowered, and the nation was now very nearly in a free trade posture.

The textile industries in Britain and France and in the German states made a much more rapid recovery than their counterpart in the United States. Thus the international cotton market resumed its expansion in 1858. Demand for the staple in 1859 and 1860 exceeded even the most optimistic expectations of southern planters and their agents. The appearance of prosperity in the South and hard times in the North did not escape influential southern observers. One of the more unfortunate effects of the Depression of 1857 was its political ramifications. It bred overconfidence among articulate southerners. Southern politicians like James H. Hammond proclaimed that "cotton is king." Similarly, conservatives and even moderates in the Republican party, dismayed by the economic malaise of the North, became less willing to challenge southern extremists on the territorial issue. After John Brown's ill-conceived raid on Harpers Ferry, for instance, many northern businessmen quailed at the threat of southern boycotts of their goods. Before all the emotional rhetoric that came in the aftermath of the raid subsided, its baneful effect was being felt in the new Thirty-sixth Congress.

For almost two months, the House was deadlocked, unable to elect a Speaker and thus go about its business. Democrats were split between the Buchanan wing and the followers of Douglas. The Republicans had a plurality of votes, but were unable to secure a majority. Nor did they have enough votes to change the majority rule as they had managed in 1857 when they elected Nathaniel P. Banks as Speaker. Even when the Republicans finally succeeded in electing William Pennington as Speaker and in organizing the House, southern and southern-leaning members of Congress were able to block all significant legislation. The Congress became little more than a debating society in which many members went to sessions armed and where insults were frequently exchanged between the more emotional spokesmen. In the midst of this atmosphere of distrust, a House committee headed by a Republican congressman from Pennsylvania, John Covode, uncovered evidence of corruption in the Buchanan administration. The distracted Democrats, in the midst of preparing for the campaign of 1860, now had to face charges of financial wrongdoing in the War Department and malfeasance in the affairs of their elected public printer.

At this point, Jefferson Davis, now a senator from Mississippi, headed a movement which he hoped would defeat Stephen A. Douglas's nomination at the Democratic party's national convention that was to be held at Charleston, South Carolina, in April 1860. What Davis sought was a caucus resolution that would bind Democratic members of Congress to vote for a national slave code. Such a resolution would be unacceptable to Douglas Democrats since among other things it completely abrogated popular sovereignty in the territories and posed a distinct threat to the free states themselves. Although Davis managed to get the resolution passed in caucus, it had no legal effect since it was simply a party measure. In that respect, however, it foretold the defeat of Douglas at Charleston and the formal division of the Democratic party along sectional lines.

The struggle over slavery in the territories seemed to draw not just opposing political lines but to begin a process, long predicted by Calhoun, where the Union was being divided into separate geographical entities. The nation was in the throes of an uneven modernizing process, with all the internal tensions that such drastic changes were imposing. Southern slave-plantation society no less than the society of the industrializing North rested on a fragile order where elitist groups jealously protected material rewards, be they manufacturers or planters, entrepreneurs or professional classes.

In the underdeveloped South there was a striking disparity of wealth between the great landowners and the small farmers and poor whites who constituted most of the nonblack and non-Indian population. Since colonial times race was the bond that held the substance of southern society together despite the unequal distribution of wealth and the inequality of opportunity among the dominant whites. But southern leadership had felt vulnerable to populist threats in the years following the Missouri controversy of 1819. Republican leadership sensed the uneasiness of the South's ruling classes and resolved to exploit it for possible gain. As the Republican national committee prepared for the campaign of 1860, it financed the publication and mass distribution of Hinton Helper's controversial book *The Impending Crisis of the South: How To Meet It.* Helper, a North Carolina representative of the yeoman or small farmer class, had written a persuasive tract condemning slavery as an uneconomic institution that degraded labor and was utilized by rich planters to monopolize the wealth of the region. While comparatively small groups of planters with moderate to large land holdings lived well and a few extravagantly, a majority of the southern population engaged in subsistence farming. It is no wonder that such antislavery propaganda provoked a strong reaction from the threatened elite. Nor is it surprising that Kansas and the formation of the Republican party should have aroused such intense feelings of insecurity among those who controlled the economy and the society of the slave states.

Unrest was also endemic in the North. Although much of the population was still engaged in farming and adhered to traditional rural values, urbanization was well advanced in the score or so of growing cities. Country to city migration was as significant as the swell of foreign immigrants during the 1840s and 1850s. Agricultural markets were becoming more specialized and more dependent on distant sources as more extensive and more efficient transportation developed. Since 1819 cycles of prosperity and depression had had a cumulative effect on northern agricultural income and output. Southern cotton producers, whose livelihood was wholly dependent on the vagaries of distant markets, felt these forces more acutely. But unemployment and social disorder in northern cities that were unprepared for the rapid influx of native and foreign populations were a source of major concern to urban and rural leadership groups. The stability of the entire social order seemed precarious. Yet as the two political parties prepared to nominate candidates for the presidency, no partisan leader could foresee how fragile the fabric of Union had become.

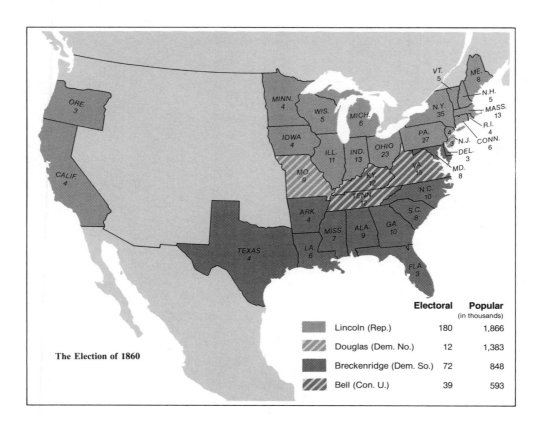

The Election of 1860

	Electoral	Popular (in thousands)
Lincoln (Rep.)	180	1,866
Douglas (Dem. No.)	12	1,383
Breckenridge (Dem. So.)	72	848
Bell (Con. U.)	39	593

CHAPTER FIVE

Disunion

As the presidential campaign of 1860 approached, the new Republican coalition, openly sectional in nature and appeal, had overcome its initial problems of organization. Under the leadership of Edwin D. Morgan, a rich New York merchant and banker, and supported by a group of reform-minded northeastern businessmen, the party had substantial financial support to mount an elaborate (for the times) presidential campaign. The Democratic party remained the only political organization that maintained a national constituency. But the tensions that had been developing since the end of the Mexican-American War and that would soon pull it apart were near the breaking point by 1860.

The Election of 1860

The fate of the party, and indeed to many, the fate of the federal Union seemed to rest upon one man, Stephen A. Douglas of Illinois. The intense and combative Douglas was the only politician of national stature who was presenting a moderate program on the slavery issue. It was still doubtful whether Douglas's popular sovereignty approach would solve the problem. Kansas, Dred Scott, John Brown, and the Lincoln-Douglas debates, if anything, pointed to a rupture between the free and the slave states.

An increasing number of opinion leaders in the slave states were advocating secession as a practical alternative. Since the formation of the republic, the doctrine of limited government and of states' rights held that separation from the Union was an option that could be exercised in a dire necessity. Calhoun and his followers had derived this theory of government from ideas that Jefferson and Madison had put forth in the Virginia and Kentucky Resolutions of 1798. An opposing view, first developed by Alexander Hamilton, reasserted by John Marshall, Daniel Webster, and Joseph Story, argued that the Union derived its legitimacy from the people, not the states, and that the Union once entered into was a perpetual compact. The new Republican party largely subscribed to the Marshall-Webster view, while acknowledging a broad spectrum of states' rights—personal liberty laws, for instance—that sought to frustrate the execution of the Fugitive Slave Act.

Southerners had threatened secession, or separation as it had been popularly called since the Missouri Compromise debates during 1819–20. Northerners tended not to take these expressions seriously. Some thoughtful persons who had kept up with events as they were unfolding did find some cause for alarm in the separationist movements in South Carolina. George Templeton Strong was one of those few who were aware of the condition of the Union. He noted that a "large and influential southern party is working hard for disunion and in South Carolina, at least, is strong enough to overawe and silence the sensible."

Words of caution like these had little effect on the general public and on many Democratic politicians who were preparing for their national convention in 1860. Douglas busied himself in perfecting his organization in the northern states.

He sought to strengthen his standing in the South, where opinion was veering away from popular sovereignty. The Buchanan administration continued to utilize its patronage strength to cripple the Douglas effort. For personal, political, and sectional reasons, a small group of senators from the North and South also joined forces to defeat his candidacy in the forthcoming party convention. They were Jesse Bright of Indiana, John Slidell, a New York–born Louisiana politician, William Bigler of Pennsylvania, and James A. Bayard of Delaware. All of them had personal grievances against Douglas and were closely associated with the administration. Jefferson Davis had already provided the ammunition for their assault on Douglas with his resolutions calling for a national slave code. If they could hold together the cotton state delegates on this extreme policy, they could defeat Douglas in the convention.

In 1856 the Democratic national committee, in a move to promote sectional harmony, selected Charleston, South Carolina, as the site for the party's 1860 convention. This decision would have grave consequences for the Douglas forces. Of all southern cities Charleston was the center of proslavery agitation. Its unpredictable late spring climate and its lack of hotel accommodations made it a poor site for a national convention. With allies like William Lowndes Yancey of Alabama, whose reputation as a southern "fire eater" was unmatched, the anti-Douglas senatorial group sought to commit a majority of the delegations from the seven southern states of Arkansas, Alabama, Florida, Georgia, Louisiana, Mississippi, and Texas to Davis's slave-code platform. If the convention went against them on this point, the strategy was to withdraw as a unit.

On April 23, 1860, the convention opened. At first it seemed that the well-disciplined Douglas organization would carry all before it. But a failure to obtain the required two-thirds vote for nomination and southern solidarity on the slave code defeated the "Little Giant." The delegates from eight southern states withdrew from the convention when they failed to have their way with the platform. Even with these anti-Douglas delegates not voting, Douglas was unable to achieve the necessary two-thirds majority after sixty ballots. He was, however, nominated at a second convention that was held in Baltimore on June 23. Herschel V. Johnson of Georgia reluctantly agreed to be named on the Douglas ticket for the vice presidency after Benjamin Fitzpatrick of Alabama declined nomination. By then, however, the Democratic party was doomed. The seceding Democrats named Buchanan's Vice President, John C. Breckinridge of Kentucky, formerly a Douglas enthusiast but now a supporter of the national slave code, for President and Joseph Lane of Oregon as his running mate. Also, on May 10 conservatives primarily from the border states had nominated John Bell of Tennessee and Edward Everett of Massachusetts on what was called the Constitutional Union ticket. This splinter party that was made up largely of former Whigs favored compromising on divisive issues that separated the free and slave states.

Viewing with satisfaction the disarray of their opponents, Republicans could now sense the possibility of victory in November. Pragmatically their leaders began moving as much toward the center on the slavery question as possible without giving up their determination to prohibit the spread of the institution into the territories. With his astute manager Thurlow Weed directing his campaign, Seward had been the strongest Republican candidate until the breakup of the Democratic party. But he was now considered too radical on the slavery question because of his refusal to return fugitive slaves while governor of New York. His tactless remark about "an irrepressible conflict" between freedom and slavery also hurt his candidacy. Like Douglas, Seward had been too long in the political limelight. He and his associate Weed had accumulated a legion of political enemies, especially among the anti-Nebraska Democrats in the Republican coalition.

Salmon P. Chase, twice elected Republican governor of the populous and important state of Ohio, formerly a Free Soil and Democratic United States senator, was also considered too radical and too opportunistic in his previous party associations. In addition he had his share of political enemies in his own state. Another candidate, Edward Bates of Missouri, an ex-Whig and Know Nothing from a border state, was certainly conservative enough. But apart from being backed by the Blair family and Horace Greeley, Bates lacked broad appeal, a strong organization, and was certain to be opposed by the immigrant vote.

Abraham Lincoln, although not as well known as either Seward or Chase, was less controversial. He, too, however had spoken in pretty bold words at the Republican convention that nominated him for the United States Senate in 1858. Taking his theme from the striking phrase in Mark 3:25, Lincoln had said, "A house divided against itself cannot stand." He had gone on to define carefully what he meant. "I believe this government cannot endure permanently half slave and half free." He was quick to add that he did not expect the Union to break up or the house to fall, but he was candid enough to predict that the republic would become "all one thing or all the other." Lincoln's advisors had thought these remarks were too radical when he asked their opinion just before he gave his speech. Only Billy Herndon, his loquacious law partner, concurred that his references to slavery were just right. Lincoln had agreed with Herndon and gave the speech as he had written it.

Convention members listened with close attention, but they did not interrupt with applause. Northern Republican editorial opinion was also restrained, while those southern newspapers that noticed it found the remarks typical of "Black Republicans" who would destroy their social and economic institutions. Douglas and the newspapers that supported him repeatedly attacked the "house divided" statement as radical and provocative. Moderate and conservative Republicans in the Midwest were disturbed by its tone. Still Lincoln's reference to the biblical injunction did not have the damaging long-range effect of Seward's careless remark. In the debates with Douglas, he had gone out of his way to proclaim himself a moderate antislavery man. At Ottawa on August 21, 1858, Lincoln had said: "I have no purpose directly or indirectly to interfere with the institution of slavery in the states where it exists. I believe I have no lawful right to do so, and I have no inclination to do so."

Within Illinois itself and in neighboring states Lincoln had the benefit of a strong local organization. After his well-publicized performance in the debates with Douglas, Lincoln had been invited to give a lecture at Henry Ward Beecher's Plymouth Congregational Church in Brooklyn, New York. Lincoln and his small group of intimate advisors saw in the invitation an opportunity to present his views and his person to the eastern Republican establishment, provided he could speak on political subjects. After Lincoln received permission to do so from the church committee, he accepted the invitation and began a careful preparation of his remarks.

Accompanied by his eldest son Robert, who was planning to attend Andover Academy in Massachusetts, Lincoln arrived in New York City on a cold February evening in 1860. He found that his speech, which had been given wide advance publicity in the New York press, had been moved from the Brooklyn church to the auditorium of the new Cooper Union Institute in what was then uptown Manhattan. Unknown to Lincoln at the time, the move and the pre-speech publicity had been deeply influenced by presidential politics. Although Lincoln was not well known in the east, Horace Greeley, William Cullen Bryant, and other Republican leaders in the city had decided at the last moment to utilize the Lincoln appearance and his speech as a further move in a campaign they were orchestrating against Seward and his political partner, Weed. They would not be disappointed.

In the midst of a driving snowstorm, over 1500 people trudged uptown and crowded into the Cooper Institute to observe this strange phenomenon from the West. And he seemed strange indeed when he rose from his chair and moved to the platform. Tall, thin, ungainly, he was dressed in a rumpled, poorly fitting black suit. When he began his remarks his voice was shrill and had more than a trace of border state drawl. But as he warmed to his subject he captured and held the attention of his audience. His message, partly directed against Douglas's continued arguments for popular sovereignty and partly directed against the extremism of the hour, was a conservative approach to national problems, but in no way a retreat from the free-soil principle. "Wrong as we think slavery is," he said, "we can yet afford to let it alone where it is, because that much is due to the necessity arising from its actual presence in the nation; but can we, while our votes will prevent it, allow it to spread into the national Territories, and to overrun us here in these free states? If our sense of duty forbids this, then let us stand by our duty fearlessly and effectively." Lincoln denied that the Republican party was a sectional party. If anything it was the southerners who had defined it as such. He condemned John Brown's raid and asserted vehemently that the Republican party was completely innocent of any complicity in it.

Lincoln's speech, suffused as it was with a deep sense of moral conviction, carefully blended a clear, realistic assessment of the problem facing the nation with the overriding importance of a peaceful solution for the future of the republic. It was an instant sensation not just with his audience, but with the thousands of readers of the *New York Tribune*, the *New York Evening Post*, and other metropolitan papers backing the Republican party in the East and the Midwest, all of which gave the speech prominent display and warm editorial support. Lincoln delivered much the same address throughout southern New England at cities and towns along the route to and from Andover. His careful and logical approach to the issue of slavery in the territories and his eloquent articulation of the moral aspects of this burning question made his name well known not just to party leaders in the East but to a much wider audience. By the time he returned to Illinois, he had moved from a dark horse candidate to one of the principal challengers of William H. Seward for the Republican nomination. The choice of Chicago as the site for the Republican convention also helped mightily in giving momentum to his budding candidacy.

Yet Seward was still the front runner when the Republican convention met a week after the Democratic convention in Charleston. The little New Yorker received 173 votes on the first ballot to 102 for Lincoln. Thereafter his support declined steadily while Lincoln's rose. On the fourth ballot Lincoln was nominated. Hannibal Hamlin, formerly an anti-Nebraska Democrat from Maine, was named for Vice President. The Republican platform was firm on its insistence that slavery be restricted to the states where it legally existed. Otherwise its rhetoric on the immorality of slavery was less strident than it had been in 1856. The platform included a call for an increase in the *ad valorem* rates of the tariff of 1857, a transcontinental railroad, and a liberal homestead act.

Republicans added color to the campaign when they utilized popular drill teams and organized bodies of young men under the catchy rubric of "The Wide Awakes," for colorful parades. Recruited from members of state militias, from volunteer fire companies like Ellsworth's famed Zouaves, or from fraternal organizations, the Wide Awakes, with their kerosene torches and their black oilcloth capes, escorted Republican campaign orators to their mass meetings. Douglas Democrats quickly copied the idea of the "Wide Awakes" with teams of "Little Giants" in the northern and midwestern states. And in the South and in border states, Breckinridge and Bell supporters enlisted similar companies of young men. The campaign of 1860 was marked with many modern electioneering tactics to spur popular enthusiasm. But among the contenders, only Douglas broke precedent and went on a speaking tour that eventually took him through twenty-three states.

Although he realized that New England was strong Republican territory, Douglas began his campaign there in the hopes that he could reunite Democratic opposition while promoting himself and his stand on popular sovereignty elsewhere. Douglas's efforts did succeed in strengthening his candidacy outside of the Northeast, but he was unable either to effect a significant fusion of his followers with the Bell and Breckinridge forces, or to make any inroads on the Republican vote. Nor was he able to create any substantial change of popular attitudes in the key states of Indiana, Ohio, and Pennsylvania, all of which held state elections a month before the presidential election in November. When Douglas learned that all of these states had gone Republican by decided majorities, he knew that Lincoln would win the presidency. Lincoln's success, he thought, would place the Union in grave danger. As he remarked at the time, "Mr. Lincoln is the next President. We must try to save the Union. I will go south." A weary, travel-worn Douglas, his health precarious from excessive work, excitement, and heavy drinking, carried the theme of Union and peaceful acceptance of Lincoln's election into the Deep South. This, his last public service, though doomed to disappointment, would be a supreme act of devotion to his nation, unblemished by any sordid personal or political motive. Speaking before frequently hostile crowds, enduring abusive treatment from an irresponsible press, Douglas insisted that there was a conspiracy to destroy the Union, but he relied on the good sense of the southern people to resist the blandishments of the secessionists.

The sectional nature of the election of 1860 was evident in the returns. Douglas, the only national candidate, won the undivided electoral vote of only one state, Missouri, though he received almost 30 percent of the popular vote. Breckinridge carried the slave states. He had a popular vote of 570,000. The Bell vote, which could be considered Unionist, trailed Breckinridge by only 55,000 votes, and if these votes were added to those for Douglas in the South, Unionism or at least moderation was surely the majority opinion of that region. Lincoln's plurality of 39 percent of the popular vote gave him a decided majority in the electoral college. He received 180 electoral votes, followed by Breckinridge with 72 votes, Bell with 39, and Douglas with 12. Lincoln did not receive one vote in the Deep South because his name did not appear on any of the ballots. Viewed superficially, the returns suggested Lincoln owned his victory to the Democratic split. In fact had all the opposition votes been united behind a single candidate, Lincoln would still have won an electoral majority. Such was the strength of the Republican coalition in its second presidential contest. Had that single candidate been the vigorous, magnetic Stephen A. Douglas, however, the result in the electoral college might have been different.

The Lower South Secedes

Southerners had promised secession if Lincoln won, but after the election only Douglas of all the candidates seemed aware of the immediate danger. Republicans, including Lincoln, persisted in discounting the threat to the Union as examples of overblown rhetoric. All were shaken out of their complacency when scarcely a month after Lincoln's election, South Carolina seceded from the Union. It was followed within two months by the secession of the entire Lower South. Except in South Carolina, whose government was firmly in the grip of a planter-dominated oligarchy, secession was accomplished only after overcoming significant opposition. Even in Alabama, the home state of that ultra "fire eater," William Lowndes Yancey, the Unionist opposition put up a strenuous battle. Eventually, however, a well-organized elite group carried Georgia, Florida, Alabama, Mississippi, Louisiana, and Texas out of the Union. Fearful of their own simmering problems with slaves, free blacks, and the landless poor whites who outnumbered them, this group of political and community leaders sought and won the allegiance of the yeoman class. They convinced these small farmers that the incoming Lincoln administration, through the patronage and other resources of the federal government, would destroy the existing power structures throughout the South, abolish slavery, and raise both landless poor whites and blacks to positions of economic and social equality.

In a widely acclaimed pamphlet, Howell Cobb elaborated on these points. He also emphasized the Republican party's attitude towards slavery, which he regarded as the linchpin that held together the southern social order. If the Republicans were right in their insistence on equality of races then, said

Cobb, "the institution of slavery as it exists in the Southern States is in direct violation of the fundamental principles of our government, and to say that they would not use all the power in their hands to eradicate the evil and restore the government to its *ancient faith*, would be to write themselves down self-convicted traitors both to principle and duty."

Since the planter-professional elite controlled the means of communication and hence community persuasion, it secured majorities in the elections for delegates to the secession conventions. In Georgia, for example, the delegates were divided between those who wanted immediate secession—primarily planters and their allies among the professional and commercial classes—and those who would postpone action until the course of the new administration could be more accurately determined. Immediate secessionists, which included the most influential people in the state, were much better organized and to a large extent controlled the information media. They also profited from the overrepresentation of the towns and cities in the nomination and election process. Moreover the immediate secessionists moved much more rapidly than the opposition.

The Georgia pattern was duplicated throughout the Lower South. It is probable that a majority of the white southern population opposed secession, but the ultras outmaneuvered them, and then in conventions that they controlled outvoted their more conservative opponents. By February 1861 all of the Lower South had seceded from the Union. At the end of that month the Provisional Confederacy had been formed at Montgomery, Alabama. Jefferson Davis was elected President, Alexander H. Stephens, formerly a Whig congressman from Georgia and an opponent of immediate secession, was named Vice President.

Buchanan and the National Crisis

Meanwhile in Washington, the Buchanan administration reacted indecisively during the early stages of the crisis. The

President's message to Congress, while it condemned secession, at the same time could find no power under the Constitution to stop it. Howell Cobb, the able but secession-minded secretary of the treasury and a Buchanan confidant, left the administration to manage the immediate secession movement in Georgia. John Floyd, secretary of war, under a cloud for his questionable dealings in his handling of Indian trust funds, resigned and returned to his native Virginia. On January 8, Jacob Thompson, secretary of the interior, also resigned and departed for his home in Mississippi. The seventy-nine year old Lewis Cass, secretary of state, who for some time had been unable to carry on the responsibilities of his office, resigned about the same time.

As the new year came around and secession was seen as an accomplished fact, two strong Unionists entered the cabinet to replace southerners who had resigned. Buchanan appointed fellow Pennsylvanian and current United States attorney general Jeremiah Sullivan Black to head the State Department. To the post Black vacated he named a resident of Washington, D.C., Edwin M. Stanton, one of the more prominent trial lawyers in the country. For the Treasury Department he selected the old Jacksonian Unionist Democrat from Kentucky, became secretary of war John A. Dix of New York. Joseph Holt, a and for the remainder of Buchanan's term acted also as secretary of the interior. These cabinet changes immediately resulted in a stiffening of the administration's policy. Buchanan refused to bow to South Carolina's demand that Major Robert Anderson, who commanded a small United States Army force at Fort Sumter in Charleston harbor, evacuate the post. The administration sent the large merchant vessel *Star of the West* with supplies for the beleaguered army unit. The *Star of the West* came under heavy fire from the South Carolina batteries that commanded the approaches to Charleston harbor. It was forced to turn back without completing its mission. Buchanan also refused to acknowledge the commissioners South Carolina sent to Washington.

While these events were taking place, Congress sought to

mediate the differences between the sections and effect a compromise. In the House, Charles Francis Adams, son and grandson of Presidents, headed a committee of thirty-three Democrats and Republicans appointed to seek some sort of adjustment that might preserve the Union. In the Senate the venerable senator from Kentucky, John Jordan Crittenden, was elected chairman of a similar bipartisan committee consisting of three northern Democrats, five Republicans, three border-state Democrats and two Democrats from the Deep South.

The deliberations of the Senate committee immediately took precedence over Adams's unwieldy counterpart in the House. Crittenden had already developed a compromise plan that proposed six constitutional amendments. But of these only one was crucial, that which extended the Missouri Compromise line to the California border "while such territory shall remain under territorial government" and explicitly made the federal government the guardian of slavery in the territories south of the Compromise line. Other amendments sought to guarantee slavery where it existed in the states. Congress was deprived of the power to act against slavery. All of these amendments and the slavery clauses in the Constitution were to be immunized against any future amendment that might be enacted to repeal or alter them in any way.

Since the Crittenden compromise line would not only decree slavery in a part of the territories but would enact a national slave code there, it went directly against the bedrock principle of the Republican party and was therefore unacceptable to Republican members of the committee. In addition, it would undercut popular sovereignty, the core belief of the Douglas Democrats. The five Republicans on the committee who had in the meantime heard from Lincoln would not accept the Compromise line, nor would the two Democrats from the cotton states after they learned of the Republican stand. The Crittenden committee began its deliberations on December 22 and reported to the Senate on December 28 that it was unable to come to any agreement. Adams's committee in the House for a time seemed on the verge of providing an acceptable formula when most of its Republican members agreed to admit New Mexico immediately as a state with no mention of slavery. But nothing came of this concession.

On Monday, January 21, 1861 a dramatic event occurred in Washington that symbolized the end of the old Union. Commencing with South Carolina in December 1860, secession conventions in the Deep South were held over the next month and five states altogether had seceded. When it was learned that Georgia had seceded on January 19, the senators from Florida, Alabama, and Mississippi resolved to announce their resignation on the Senate floor in concert to achieve the maximum dramatic effect. The Washington press announced the time and place of the event and as a result the galleries of the Senate were completely jammed. It was estimated that a thousand spectators had gathered to witness what all felt would be an historic occasion.

David L. Yulee of Florida led off with a brief, emotion-packed speech. He was followed by his colleague, Florida senator Stephen K. Mallory, and then the handsome Clement C. Clay of Alabama and his colleague Benjamin Fitzpatrick. After Fitzpatrick had declared that his loyalty to his state transcended any loyalty to the United States, Jefferson Davis rose and made a brief address. He had been ill the night before and at first his voice faltered. But it gained strength as he proceeded. "I am sure I feel no hostility to you, Senators of the North," he said. "I am sure there is not one of you, whatever sharp discussion there may have been between us, to whom I cannot now say, in the presence of my God, I wish you well." After each speech, the galleries exploded with emotion. "At times," recalled an observer, "the Sergeant-at-Arms was ordered to clear the galleries, a duty he did not perform." At the conclusion of Davis's remarks, his colleagues rose from their desks and forming behind Senator Yulee marched in single file out of the chamber. "There was everywhere a feeling of suspense," another contemporary observer wrote, "as if, visibly, the pillars of the temple were being withdrawn and the great Government structure was tottering."

The Republicans, including their leader Abraham Lincoln, still believed that a moderate majority in the South would curb the ultras. By offering federal guarantees to preserve slavery in the present slave-owning states, they felt that the Provisional Confederacy would dissolve. After all Virginia, North Carolina, Tennessee, Kentucky, Arkansas, Missouri, Maryland, and Delaware still remained in the Union. And without these powerful and populous border states, could the cotton states survive and prosper? Delay was the policy that the new administration adopted, but delay played into the hands of the secessionists, who seized the initiative in Virginia and other border states as they had in the secession conventions of December and January.

Yet the Unionists maintained a slender majority in the Virginia legislature. This majority proposed a final measure to head off the rupture of the Union. Sponsored by ex-President John Tyler, the Virginia legislature sent out a call for a conference composed of delegates from all the states to meet in Washington on February 4, 1861. None of the already seceded states answered the invitation. Moreover the Tyler proposal was regarded with considerable skepticism in the North. Most of the northern states sent delegations, but their power to negotiate was strictly limited. Some 132 delegates met at Willard's Hotel, where they debated various compromise plans until February 27, when the convention adjourned. It was dubbed "the Old Gentlemen's Convention" because a majority of its members were of mature years and no longer active in politics. The Peace Conference issued a report that largely duplicated the defunct proposals of the Crittenden Compromise.

By the time the Peace Conference report was presented to Congress, the Provisional Confederacy was in operation. Property of the federal government in the Lower South such as mints, forts, customs houses, and arsenals had already been seized by either state or Confederate authorities. While Lincoln was en route to Washington in late February, only two important posts in the Confederacy flew the Stars and Stripes and both were in jeopardy. They were Fort Sumter in Charleston harbor and Fort Pickens, located on an island off the Florida coast at Pensacola. Confederate commissioners were in Washington and agents of the new government were active in all the border states.

On February 11 the President-elect left Springfield for Washington following a circuitous route that took him through Cincinnati, Pittsburgh, Cleveland, Buffalo, Albany, New York, and Philadelphia, almost 2,000 miles over some twenty different railroad lines. Traveling in the sealed car and enduring the many stops for changes (over twenty in Ohio alone) in the dead of winter, Lincoln, it would seem, needlessly put up with hardship and expenditure of energy. He had given no public speeches during the campaign and in fact had not left Springfield since his nomination, but he made up for his silence by offering brief remarks wherever any group of the curious, be they well-wishers or opponents, might gather when the train stopped for fuel, water, or to change locomotives. At the various cities along his route in the Midwest, New York state, and Pennsylvania, he delivered speeches. Reporters and politicians who sought to find clues to his policy in his comments were baffled. All that could be determined with some degree of certainty was that the President-elect was committed to preserving the Union. But whether he would go to war for this purpose was unclear because he constantly emphasized his belief in a peaceful solution of the nation's problems. Republican leaders, as they read accounts of the long, slow journey, wrung their hands. After the cavalcade reached Philadelphia, Lincoln received warnings from General Scott and Seward of an assassination plot. He canceled an appearance in Harrisburg and slipped through Baltimore to Washington, where a suite at Willard's Hotel awaited him.

When Lincoln reached Washington, he had settled on only two cabinet positions, state and attorney general. For the State

Department he had selected his formidable rival for the nomination, William H. Seward. Attorney general went to another rival, Edward Bates. Between February 23 and March 5 he filled all the other posts. For the War Department he chose Simon Cameron. Montgomery Blair became postmaster general. Salmon P. Chase was appointed Secretary of the Treasury. Caleb Smith, who had been instrumental in swinging the Indiana vote to Lincoln at a crucial moment in the Republican convention, was named secretary of the interior. And Gideon Welles, who had also played a key role in the Chicago convention, received the Navy Department.

Lincoln's appointment policy reflected both sectional and political imperatives. Seward had been the most prominent Whig politician in the country and of course represented New York, the most populous and wealthiest state in the Union. Chase had been a Democrat and was accounted a radical on the slavery issue. His state, Ohio, was third in the nation in population and material resources. Cameron represented Pennsylvania and the anti-Nebraska Democrats in the Republican coalition, as did Gideon Welles and Montgomery Blair. Bates and Smith had both been Whigs. Thus the cabinet lineup contained three who had been Whigs and three who had been Democrats. Two of the members, Bates and Blair, represented important border states, Missouri and Maryland. Seward, Cameron, and Welles were spokesmen for the interests of the Middle Atlantic states and New England. Smith and the President himself were westerners who had been Whigs while the Vice President, Hannibal Hamlin, was an anti-Nebraska Democrat from Maine.

War Begins

Before cabinet matters were settled, Lincoln, who had already prepared a draft of his inaugural address, turned it over to Seward for his comments. While the hawk-nosed Seward was studying Lincoln's draft, a delegation of Virginia Unionists met with the President-elect. They apprized him of the tense situation in their state. The Washington Peace Conference had just adjourned without any acceptable solution to the crisis. Seward, for whom Lincoln had a great deal of respect, had emerged as one of the leading compromisers in the Republican leadership ranks. Along with his associate Weed, Seward believed that negotiation and delay would strengthen Unionist sentiment in the South to such an extent that some modest concessions would reunite the nation. After indirect contacts with the Confederate commissioners then in Washington, Seward urged Lincoln to adopt a conciliatory posture. His influence can be noted by comparing Lincoln's original draft of the inaugural address with the one that he delivered on March 4.

The border states, particularly Virginia, claimed the immediate attention of both Lincoln and Jefferson Davis. Virginia, the Old Dominion as it was affectionately termed, was not only the most populous of the slave states, but it had in addition considerable industrial capacity. Its prestige with the nation and especially the South was immense. The state of Washington and Jefferson, of Madison, Monroe, and of Patrick Henry, Virginia seemed the very embodiment of patriotic heritage and republican virtue. Maryland too was both a strategic and material prize. Baltimore was the fourth largest port in the nation. An impressive manufacturing infrastructure had grown up in and around the city, which was the hub for two important rail lines, the Baltimore and Ohio and the Pennsylvania. Indeed, Washington was completely surrounded by Maryland and Virginia; they controlled the capital city's communications with the North and the West. If Virginia should secede, North Carolina would go too and so probably would Tennessee. Missouri, Maryland, Delaware, and Arkansas might remain in the Union or join the Confederacy. All of these border slave states had active secessionist groups in their governments and their press. If all of the border slave states sided with the Confederacy, Washington would be cut off from the Union and the new Lincoln administration placed in grave danger. But more important than even the loss of the capital city were the human and material resources the border states would bring to the Confederacy. At stake were the eight slave states of the Upper South that had a population of 7,271,152—about one fourth of the nation's total population. In material resources, Virginia and Maryland had the Union's largest iron-rolling mills. Missouri and Kentucky were the leading breeders of horses and mules. Other border slave states contained valuable mineral deposits, important for any economy.

On the other hand, if all the border states remained in the Union the Provisional Confederacy would be in dire straits. In all likelihood, it would be forced into submission after a comparatively short interval. This consideration influenced the policy of the Union and the Confederacy as they maneuvered to secure the allegiance of the vital border region. Warned repeatedly that any hostile act against the Confederacy would result in the secession of Virginia and probably North Carolina, Lincoln went as far as he felt he could to reassure Virginia's convention, then in session at Richmond, that he would not use force to recover government property that the seceding states had seized prior to his inauguration. Although he spoke in broad terms that gave him considerable latitude in dealing with the seceded states, he made it quite clear that the government would defend Fort Pickens and Fort Sumter should they be attacked.

During the first month of his administration, Lincoln had been of two minds on Sumter. He had received word that Major Anderson was short of supplies and in fact after April 15 would have no rations left for his tiny, makeshift garrison. Responding to the counsel of his postmaster general, Montgomery Blair, Lincoln authorized Blair's brother-in-law, former naval officer Gustavus Vasa Fox, to prepare a relief expedition to Sumter. The situation at Pickens was thought to be more secure. Men and supplies had been dispatched to that post in the closing days of the Buchanan administration. In addition Fort Pickens was easier to defend than Sumter, which was completely flanked by Confederate batteries. Obviously the new administration had committed itself to keeping the flag flying in the Confederacy.

With the border state problem uppermost in his mind, Lincoln temporized during early April 1861. His military commander, General Winfield Scott, advised him that Sumter could not be defended and that Anderson's garrison should be withdrawn. Scott also stressed the unpreparedness of the Union for any conflict. Seward joined Scott in urging that Sumter be evacuated and argued that if a stand be made it ought to be at Fort Pickens. But when Lincoln received information that Pickens had not been strengthened as had been thought, because of a conflict of orders between the Navy Department and the War Department, and that the fort might even be in Confederate hands, he made up his mind to provision Sumter. And he decided to give the South Carolina authorities notice to that effect. Accordingly he drafted instructions for a messenger, who left for Charleston on April 6. In the messenger's instructions was the notification to Governor Francis Pickens of South Carolina. The messenger was directed to read the following statement to the governor: "an attempt will be made to supply Fort Sumpter [sic] with provisions only, and that, if such an attempt be not resisted, no effort to throw in men, arms, or ammunition, will be made, without further notice, or in case of an attack on the Fort."

On April 8 the messenger arrived in Charleston and read the notification to the governor, who in turn gave it to P. G. T. Beauregard, commanding general in Charleston. After Beauregard received confirmation from one of the Confederate commissioners in Washington that the notice was genuine, he telegraphed his government in Montgomery. The Confederate secretary of war, speaking for the government, ordered him to demand evacuation of the fort, and if refused, Beauregard was authorized to use force. Seward, still determined to avert what he felt would be imminent conflict, tried to sabotage the Fox expedition, a move that was only partially successful. He managed to detach the expedition's only heavy warship, the USS *Powhatan*, which was sent to Pickens, but he was unable to halt the expedition. The remainder of the little relief fleet left

New York on April 10 and reached the vicinity of Charleston harbor at 3 AM on April 12, 1861.

Meanwhile Anderson had informed Beauregard that he would defend the fort, but that if the Confederate forces did not open hostilities, he was so short of food he would be starved out in a few days. When the Confederate cabinet learned that Anderson would run out of food and would abandon the fort by April 15, Davis and his colleagues ordered Beauregard not to take any hostile action. The arrival of Fox's relief fleet outside of Charleston harbor, however, changed their minds, though not without some painful discussion in which the big, masterful Georgian, Robert Toombs, Confederate secretary of state, took issue with Davis and his colleagues. Toombs had been pacing the floor while the cabinet discussed the Sumter crisis. When Davis announced his decision to authorize an attack on the fort, Toombs objected in rather oracular terms. "Mr. President," he said, looking directly at the thin, high-strung Davis, "at this time, it is suicide, murder, and will lose us every friend at the North. You will wantonly strike a hornet's nest which extends from mountains to ocean and legions, now quiet, will swarm out and sting us to death. It is unnecessary; it puts us in the wrong; it is fatal." But Davis felt there was no alternative, and despite Toombs's warning, carried his cabinet with him.

Anderson was handed the Confederate ultimatum. When he refused to surrender, the batteries surrounding the fort were ordered to stand ready. At 4:30 AM on April 12, 1861, a signal shell was fired from Fort Johnson, one of the Confederate batteries on the mainland opposite Sumter. By 5 AM the bombardment became general. At 7 AM Sumter returned fire. But after sustaining thirty-three hours of shelling and with portions of the fort ablaze, Anderson surrendered. Fox's ships, which were standing off the harbor, were permitted to embark Anderson and his men and transport them north.

Lincoln and Seward had hoped that Virginia would stay in the Union. The President had vetoed the Navy Department's request to reinforce the Norfolk Navy Yard because he felt it would promote uneasiness in that state. But when Lincoln reversed his cautious policy after the surrender of Major Anderson and called upon the states to provide 75,000 troops to put down a rebellion consisting of "combinations . . . too powerful to be suppressed by the ordinary course of judicial proceedings," Virginia acted promptly to secede. The Virginia convention passed an ordinance of secession on April 17. One week later it joined the Confederacy. Similar actions occurred in Arkansas, North Carolina, and Tennessee, all of which had seceded by May 1861. After two armed clashes between Unionists and secessionists, Missouri remained in the Union. Kentucky declared its neutrality. The Lincoln administration, however, acted to support the Unionists in that state. When a Confederate army under General Leonidas Polk invaded Kentucky in the late summer of 1861, the legislature affirmed its support of the Union. Maryland and Delaware both remained in the Union, though the Lincoln administration had to adopt some forceful measures to control secessionist elements in Baltimore.

Although the border state governments of Kentucky, Maryland, Delaware, and Missouri sided with the Union and Virginia, Tennessee, and Arkansas with the Confederacy, there were divisions within all of these states. Volunteer regiments from Kentucky, Maryland, and Missouri served with the Confederate armed forces. Eastern Tennessee was consistently loyal to the Union as was western Virginia. Missouri too was the scene of bitter internecine warfare. In general neither the Union nor the Confederacy was able to claim total allegiance from any of the border states, a factor that unquestionably lengthened the war.

And so the division of the nation, whose beginnings could be perceived as far back as the Missouri debates over slavery some forty years earlier, had finally come to pass. The institution of slavery precipitated the conflict because it stood in the way of a modernizing process that was changing the character not just of the United States but of the entire Western world. The liberal reform movements of the first half of the nineteenth century in western Europe and the United States introduced moral and cultural attitudes that sought to adapt society to the new efficiency and rationalism of the machine age. In this process slavery had become an anachronism, but the society based on this institution refused to go away. It took American political leaders almost half a century to face this fact, and by then it was too late to alter the deep-seated systems of the North and South without conflict.

BIBLIOGRAPHICAL EXPLANATIONS

Eyewitness Accounts

The opinions of contemporary observers who wrote of the condition of the Union during the Buchanan administration have colored much of the historical literature on the causes of the Civil War. Both northern and southern commentators had come to the conclusion that the Compromise of 1850 had been only a truce between the two sections, that the federal Union was drifting towards destruction. For a brief period after the passage of the divisive Kansas-Nebraska Act, the Democratic party sought to defuse the sectional crisis and maintain national political unity. But not one month after the election of the Democrat James Buchanan to the presidency, John Murray Forbes, the Massachusetts businessman, wrote to a southern acquaintance in words that foretold the strife to come. Forbes said that "fifteen or twenty years ago the abolition men and women were mobbed everywhere . . . now the mobs are all the other way, but it is not that they have become abolitionists. The wrong of slavery preached to them by the press, doubtless weigh with the masses, but all other influences sink into insignificance compared with that brought to bear for the two years past. . . . to convince the laboring classes here of the aristocratic nature of the institution of slavery, of the small number of slaveholders compared with the white population north and south, and of the coming issue being whether this small class (supposed to rule the south) shall own half the senate and shall use the national arm to extend their institution at home and abroad." Articulate northerners like Forbes were as fearful of aggressive tendencies to expand slavery as articulate southerners who feared a northern campaign to weaken and destroy their slave-based society.

More radical members of the newly formed Republican party were as frank as southern fire eaters about the sectional thrust of their party. Although Republicans insisted that their platform sought only to prevent slavery's spread to the territories, they did not conceal their hostility to the peculiar institution. William H. Seward of New York in a widely publicized speech saw an "irrepressible conflict" between freedom and slavery. Abraham Lincoln likened the nation to a house divided. But he made it clear in this and subsequent speeches that he thought the principle of freedom would eventually unify the nation.

Other contemporary observers in the North felt somewhat differently. William Tecumseh Sherman, one of the Union's great field commanders in the Civil War, was certain that there would be a peaceful resolution to the controversy. Writing his brother John on March 20, 1856, Sherman said, "Kansas will be a free state, so will Missouri and Kentucky in time. . . . self interest is the great motor and the Kentuckians and Missourians, seeing the land and property of adjoining free states commanding a high and ready price in consequence of the influx of white men, will feel that they have other interests besides slave property, and this cause is now telling and will go on increasing."

Stephen A. Douglas, the last of the intersectional champions, believed that a conspiracy of southern politicians engineered his defeat. The plotters, Douglas maintained, were bent on destroying the Union by dividing the Democratic party and thus assuring the election of Abraham Lincoln to the presidency on a northern antislavery platform. Douglas had made his position plain in a series of speeches and had confided his fears to Gideon Welles just before the Confederate attack on Fort Sumter. Welles elaborated on the conspiracy thesis in a series of influential articles he wrote on the Lincoln administration, which were published in *The Galaxy* in September and October 1876 and in January 1877. Specific information can be found in *The Diary of Gideon Welles*, vol. 1, ed. John T. Morse, Jr. (New York, 1911) or the modern edition by Howard K. Beale and Alan W. Brownsword, eds. (New York, 1960).

Before the Welles diary made public his supposedly authoritative evidence of a southern political conspiracy, several works of northern authors charged that former Confederate leaders had been plotting treason as early as the outbreak of the Mexican-American War in 1846. Horace Greeley's widely read two-volume work, *The American Conflict* (Hartford, Conn., 1867), vied with John Smith Dye's *The Adder's Den* (New York, 1864) in expounding this view for a popular audience in the North. But the fullest expression of the conspiracy thesis, written in a climate of post war northern nationalism, was the work of Henry Wilson, the Massachusetts Republican senator and Vice President of the United States during Grant's second administration. In his lengthy work *The History of the Rise and Fall of the Slave Power in America*, 3 vols. (Boston, 1872–1877), Wilson found a small group of southern political leaders and slave owners responsible for precipitating the war. Wilson's approach was entirely polemical and adversarial. The North was the embodiment of Union and nation, the South guilty of treason and separation on behalf of slavery. Despite its one-sided stridency, Wilson's argument received scholarly support from the trained historian Herman von Holst, whose multivolume *Constitutional and Political History of the United States*, 8 vols. (Chicago, 1876–1897), presented substantial documentary evidence to support his contention that the war came as a result of a slaveholding conspiracy to destroy the Union.

Contemporary historical literature on the causes of the Civil War from a northern viewpoint was countered by the two top southern leaders, Jefferson Davis, former President of the Confederacy, and Alexander H. Stephens, former Vice President. Davis's *The Rise and Fall of the Confederate Government*, 2 vols. (New York, 1881), a rather dense work, delved into antebellum politics and theory to argue that secession was a perfectly legitimate constitutional means of redressing grievances. Alexander H. Stephens's *Constitutional View of the Late War Between the States*, 2 vols. (Philadelphia, 1868–1870), was a fuller and more scholarly statement, but its evidence and its conclusions were similar to those of Davis. The diminutive Stephens had a better understanding of the constitutional ramifications that preceded the conflict than Davis, but he was just as firm in an apologist for the Confederate cause.

These two defenses of the southern position, however, were buried under a spate of works that promoted northern nationalism and proclaimed slavery to be the evil cause of the war, an interpretation that persisted until the turn of the century. Multivolume works like James Schouler's *History of the United States of America Under the Constitution*, 7 vols. (New York, 1880–1913) as well as single-volume monographs like John W. Burgess's *The Middle Period* (New York, 1897), arraigned the intersectional parties of the antebellum period for not taking a forthright antislavery stand. Like Wilson, Greeley, and other spokespersons for the Union cause, they found slavery to be the dominant issue. Moderate Whig and Democratic leaders of the prewar period such as Martin Van Buren, Henry Clay, James K. Polk, and especially Stephen A. Douglas were characterized as instruments of the southern slave-plantation interest.

Slavery as the principal cause of the war found its last and perhaps its most persuasive exposition in James Ford Rhodes's monumental *History of the United States from the Compro-*

mise of 1850, 7 vols. (New York, 1893–1906). Rhodes resurrected Seward's "irrepressible conflict" and made it his theme. Slavery was not only an immoral institution, but it transcended all other disputes between the sections. Thus the war was inevitable. The eventual victory of the Union was an appropriate conclusion to differences that could not be settled by peaceful means. But even as Rhodes's highly readable and scholarly volumes were coming off the press, his interpretation and the entire northern nationalist canon were being subjected to critical scrutiny.

The First Revisionists: The Dunning School

William A. Dunning, a New Jersey–born professor of history at Columbia, inaugurated the first revisionist school that challenged what had become the conventional view of events leading to the war. His *Essays on the Civil War and Related Topics* (New York, 1898) and his monograph, *Reconstruction, Political and Economic, 1865–1877* (New York, 1907), established his reputation as the leading American historian of his generation and attracted southern-born students to his seminars. His most influential student, Georgia-born and educated Ulrich Bonnell Phillips, made the study of plantation slavery his specialty. Phillips moved away from moral arguments and concentrated on the economic and social aspects of antebellum plantation life. His work dominated the study of slavery and of the antebellum south during the 1920s. His *American Negro Slavery* (New York, 1918), followed by *Life and Labor in the Old South* (Boston, 1929), did much to counteract the widely accepted abolitionist view of slavery as a moral outrage and a physically cruel, barbarous, and inhuman institution.

Phillips was the first trained historian to study plantation records, and thus his findings were buttressed by the authority of primary source material. Yet the way he shaped his evidence and the conclusions he drew reflected a regional and cultural bias. Phillips's interpretation portrayed slavery as a much more benign institution than had been previously thought.

With an array of economic evidence, he declared that not just the human, paternalist attitudes in antebellum southern customs and culture stayed the hand of all but those few planters who were cruel or harsh to their slaves, but that good management required that slaves be well treated. His books *American Negro Slavery* and *Life and Labor in the Old South* were built upon extensive research in plantation records and on the observations of the antebellum newspaperman Frederick Law Olmstead. Olmstead's three books, *Journey Through the Seaboard Slave States* (New York, 1856) *Journey Through Texas* (New York, 1857) and *Journey in the Back Country* (New York, 1860), all declared that slavery was an inefficient labor system. He had confidently predicted it would die out. Phillips confirmed Olmstead's findings in this respect. But Phillips, a southerner, reasserted the idea that slavery, though uneconomic, had remained in place until 1865 because it was the only method southern leaders could devise for maintaining social control.

An elaboration of Dunning's revisionism gave new impetus to southern history and the efforts of several scholars of southern origin to reexamine the causes of the war. William E. Dodd was the midwestern counterpart of Dunning. Devoted to the political ideals of Jefferson and of Woodrow Wilson, Dodd championed the revisionist viewpoint. Like Dunning, he received his professional training in Germany and conveyed to his students a dedication to well-researched narrative history. Dodd's specialty was the politics and the culture of the Old South as described in *The Cotton Kingdom* (New Haven, 1919) and *The Old South* (New York, 1937) for example. He communicated his scholarly interests to an unusually receptive audience.

The enthusiasm that Dodd imparted for what might be termed southern culture and its distinct way of life made a lasting impression on his students. They joined with Dunning's students to argue that some if not all of the responsibility for the conflict must be assigned to the North. Charles W. Ramsdell, like Phillips a Dunning student, spent much of his professional life building a case against northern politicians and abolitionists. Ramsdell was the first trained historian who marshalled documentary evidence that pointed to Lincoln's responsibility for maneuvering the Confederacy into firing the first shot at Fort Sumter. He presented his findings in an article he wrote for *The Journal of Southern History* 3 (1937) entitled "Lincoln and Fort Sumter."

Ramsdell's southern orientation was restrained when compared to that of Frank Owsley, who had studied with Dodd. Owsley held deeply felt beliefs that the northern historical canon had maligned the South and its role in precipitating the conflict. He supported his argument with Charles Beard's analysis of American civilization that emphasized economic forces in determining American values. In two influential articles, "The Irrepressible Conflict" in *I'll Take My Stand* (New York, 1930,) and "The Fundamental Cause of the Civil War: Egocentric Sectionalism," *The Journal of Southern History* 7 (1941), Owsley utilized Beard's model of an industrializing, bourgeois North in conflict with an agrarian South. Beard's view of the Civil War, expressed in his *Rise of American Civilization* (New York, 1927), was that the institution of slavery was simply an aspect of the larger agrarian culture that was under attack from the industrial revolution in the North. The war itself, which he called "the second American Revolution," was not fought on moral grounds, but over such points of conflict between the sections as the efficiency of slavery as a labor system, tariff policy, balance of payments, public land policy, banking, currency, public credit, and railroad development.

Owsley was not alone among the revisionists who saw the war as a conflict between two economic systems. He was, however, an outspoken defender of the southern position in 1861, and indeed came very close to restating the Confederate case that Jefferson Davis and Alexander Stephens had made seventy years before. Economic determinism in Owsley's analysis became a justification for the agrarian way of life and a harsh criticism of industrialization. Significantly Owsley thought that the argument over the moral issue of slavery was without substance. To him, slavery was a means of race adjustment and an essential part of the southern labor force in the antebellum plantation economy. Owsley was the most prominent and the most extreme apologist for the southern position among historians on responsibility for the Civil War.

The broad scholarly and eventually popular influence of Dunning, Phillips, and their students extended far beyond the study of slavery. During the 1930s and 1940s revisionist historians who had the skill to present their cases in vivid narrative and who could appeal to wide and varied audiences rather effectively revised the historical canon of the post-Civil War era.

George Fort Milton, an Indiana journalist but also a careful historian who consulted primary source material, condemned the "irrepressible conflict" thesis in his sympathetic biography of Stephen Douglas entitled *The Eve of Conflict: Stephen A. Douglas and the Needless War* (Boston, 1934). So long the object of caustic criticism as the author of the Kansas-Nebraska Act and as a politician whose only goal had been his driving ambition for the presidency, Douglas was now cast as the last Unionist. Milton described Douglas's role from 1858 to 1861 as one of moderation and defense of the intersectional party system. Had Douglas not been betrayed by a small group of political freebooters at the Democratic convention in 1860, the party would have remained intact. Douglas would have been elected President and the Union preserved.

Also from Indiana was Claude Bowers, a man whose training and career were similar to Milton's. He wrote in the revisionist tradition for a popular as well as professional audience. His work, however, was far more partisan than that of his fellow Hoosier. Bowers's *Party Battles of the Jacksonian Period* (Boston, 1922) and *The Tragic Era: The Revolution After Lincoln* (Cambridge, 1929) held up those politicians and statesmen of the Jacksonian-Democratic persuasion as the true heroes of American democracy. Whigs and Republicans who came later were cast as the enemy. Slavery in Milton's and

Bowers's estimation was a minor factor in the coming of the Civil War except when abolitionists and later radical Republicans distorted the issue for partisan reasons. But they did not glorify the "lost cause" of the Confederacy and felt no particular identity with the Democratic politics of the Solid South. Neither Milton nor Bowers rejected the theory that the sectional impulses of the North and the South were prime causes of the conflict.

Modern Revisionists

Thereafter revisionists of note interjected a more balanced view, though they were still influenced by Beard to some extent and critical of the "irrepressible conflict" thesis. Avery Craven, a Dunning student and for many years a professor of history at the University of Chicago, analyzed the burgeoning conflict between the two sections in his *Coming of the Civil War*, which was first published in 1942 (revised, New York, 1957). Craven de-emphasized sectional differences, which he saw as a natural outgrowth of a rural and an industrial society. Slavery was necessary for maintaining social order, although its economic value was important also. Craven looked elsewhere for responsibility and found it in a generation of inept politicians both North and South and in propaganda inspired by irresponsible abolitionists.

James G. Randall, the other leading revisionist historian of the 1940s and 1950s, made a similar argument but if anything he was more critical than Craven of political leadership during the antebellum years. To Randall this period was a time when a blundering generation dictated national affairs. The war was a tragic error that could and should have been avoided. This theme is evident in the early chapters of his *The Civil War and Reconstruction*, coauthored with David Herbert Donald (Lexington, Mass., 1969), and his *Lincoln, The President*, 4 vols. (New York, 1945–1955.) (Randall died before he completed the work; Richard Current wrote the last volume.) Randall's distinct antiwar interpretation led historiographers to consider his work to be a product of post–World War I disillusionment. But Kenneth Stampp, in a brilliant essay on the causes of the war in *The Imperiled Union* (New York, 1980), has pointed out quite correctly that Randall, far from being an antiwar crusader, was a stalwart backer of American intervention in both world wars. He was, in addition, an opponent of the America First isolationist movement and a firm supporter of American participation in the League of Nations and the United Nations.

Both Craven and Randall touched on mass psychological behavior as a source for the growth of sectional animosity. Roy F. Nichols, who subscribed to the needless war thesis, offered the fullest examination of this area of inquiry. In his *Disruption of American Democracy* (New York, 1948), Nichols described and analyzed the disintegration of the Democratic party between 1857 and 1860. He criticized politicians for their role in defeating Douglas at the 1860 Charleston convention and thereby destabilizing the only remaining major intersectional institution that held the Union together. But Nichols placed particular emphasis on what he labeled the "hyperemotionalism" of the period. Enumerating cohesive and divisive factors in American culture, Nichols concluded that imperfect party machinery could not contain the volatile elements that had been mounting in society since the Mexican-American War.

Kenneth Stampp, however, has made the most recent and perhaps the most compelling case for the revisionists. In his book *And The War Came: The North and the Secession Crisis 1860–1861* (Baton Rouge, 1950), Stampp admitted that cultural differences existed between the North and the South. He also concluded that many of these points of conflict were extremely deep-rooted and would have required inspired leadership for any lasting compromise. Stampp was in general agreement with Randall's and Craven's argument that inept leadership of the "blundering generation was a major factor." Nevertheless he posed the question of whether a peaceful separation of the two value systems might not have been preferable to the terrible conflict that followed. And he castigated political leaders north and south for permitting the situation between the sections to worsen to such a point that separation was the only alternative to war.

Attempts at Synthesis

As the previous discussion has indicated, revisionism held sway during the 1930s and 1940s. But still there were many contradictions and conflicting interpretations of the causes of the war when Allan Nevins brought out his *Ordeal of the Union*, 2 vols. (New York, 1947) and *The Emergence of Lincoln*, 2 vols. (New York, 1950). Nevins sought a synthesis which would do justice to the southern argument and yet at the same time give a balanced view of the slavery issue. Like Rhodes and other historians of the northern nationalist school, Nevins regarded slavery as the prime cause of the conflict. But as a northerner and a midwesterner, he emphasized the cause of national unification that foreshadowed Lincoln's role in maintaining the Union. He condemned slavery as a moral iniquity, but he restated Phillips's thesis on race adjustment in the South. Likewise Nevins accepted Olmstead's and Phillips's opinion that slavery was a backward institution when compared with the free labor ethos of the North. Similarly the psychological interpretation that Craven, Randall, and especially Nichols had advanced was skillfully interwoven in his vivid narrative. The personalities of Stephen A. Douglas at the time of the Kansas-Nebraska Act and John Brown when he made his ill-fated assault on the federal arsenal at Harpers Ferry were both subjects of psychological evaluation. Nevins failed to achieve the synthesis he sought, but his vast work represents the most balanced view of the developing crisis from the conclusion of the Mexican-American War to the attack on Fort Sumter.

Arthur Schlesinger, Jr., writing in the *Christian Science Monitor* (October 14, 1950), criticized Nevins's work because it sided with the revisionists in treating abolitionists as irresponsible agents who promoted sectional tensions. Nevins had condemned fanaticism on both sides of the slavery issue and had equated abolitionists with southern fire eaters as contributors to the overheated political atmosphere. Oscar Handlin, whose review of *Ordeal of the Union* and *The Emergence of Lincoln* appeared in *The Nation* (Dec. 2, 1950), attacked Nevins's work along similar lines. Both historians were urban northerners and Harvard-trained. Fanaticism on behalf of freedom, they charged, was quite a different thing from fanaticism on behalf of slavery.

For precisely opposite reasons Nevins's attempt to achieve a balanced view of the origins of the conflict received hostile treatment from southern historians. The belief in an "irrepressible conflict" was much in evidence in Fletcher Green's review which appeared in *The Mississippi Valley Historical Review* 35 (1948). To Green and other southern historians, Nevins's work suffered from its moral bias, from its vindication of free-soil politics in the *Emergence of Lincoln* volumes, and from its highly unfavorable view of southern politicians. On the other hand James G. Randall, in the *New York Times Review of Books* (October 12, 1947), and John Hicks in the *American Historical Review* 53 (1948) both praised the Nevins volumes, though for different reasons. Randall thought Nevins's efforts to present a southern as well as a northern case were judicious, while Hicks was impressed with the implicit Rhodesian morality thesis.

Clearly no consensus had been reached on the responsibility for the war, no synthesis had been achieved. Revisionism of the Randall and Nichols sort has continued to make a mark on scholarly interpretations of the causes of the Civil War. Twenty years after the publication of Nevins's volumes, David Potter's *The Impending Crisis, 1848–1861* (New York, 1976) was published. Potter died before his masterful work was completed. His colleague at Stanford, Don E. Fehrenbacher, wrote the last two chapters and prepared the book for press. Potter's interpretation of Lincoln's debates with Douglas has not been and possibly never will be improved upon. His account of the political turmoil of the 1850s is fresh and compelling. Though he does not spare the political actors north and south, he is less critical of the blundering generation than a Randall or a Craven. Yet "the needless war" concept is an underlying thesis, and he deplores the failure of compromise which he believed possible throughout the decade prior to the war. *The Impending Crisis* along with Nevins's *Ordeal of the Union* volumes will remain for many years to come the best treatment of the causes of the war.

Sociocultural Explanations

An explicit return to "irrepressible conflict" was given new credence during the civil rights agitation from 1950 through the 1970s. Eric Foner, in his *Free Soil, Free Labor, Free Men: The Ideology of the Republican Party Before the Civil War* (New York, 1970), argued eloquently that the free labor ethic was closely related to the antislavery movement. In a forceful restatement of the sociocultural explanation for the increasing political tensions that followed the Mexican-American War, Foner saw the Republican party as the expression of bourgeois capitalism that strenuously opposed the restraints the slave-plantation South seemed to be applying to national industrial development. Thus Foner molded "the irrepressible conflict" with all its determinist implications into the breakup of intersectional parties and the emergence of differing value systems. Armed conflict between the two cultures was the only conclusion that could be drawn from such sectional antagonism. Foner has amplified his interpretation in a series of essays entitled *Politics and Ideology in the Age of the Civil War* (New York, 1980). He has not lacked for critics, however.

In a book that broke new ground on the southern roots of the war, William W. Freehling saw the genesis of the conflict in the nullification crisis in South Carolina. See his *Prelude to Civil War: The Nullification Controversy in South Carolina, 1816–1836* (New York, 1968). But see also Richard Ellis, *The Union at Risk: Jacksonian Democracy, States' Rights, and the Nullification Crisis* (New York, 1987).

Another group of modern scholars has taken sharp exception to such sectional and determinist approaches. Influenced by recent trends in the study of history that stress quantification of data where the computer has made possible the analysis of enormous quantities of statistical material, these social historians have concentrated on the grass roots aspects of political behavior. Their insistence that the only proper dimension of historical scholarship is the analysis of mass behavior, whether it be in politics or in culture, has led them to scorn all work that does not conform to their interpretation of history. Such phrases as "traditional," "impressionist," "old fashioned," or "elitist" figure prominently in their vocabulary. They refer to their approach that emphasizes and classifies the prewar social milieu, as the "new" social or "new" political history from an "ethnocultural" viewpoint. The religious fervor which characterized the prewar period (and the postwar period for that matter) is an important subject of their studies. Accordingly they have taken the religious revivalism of the Second Great Awakening and have broken it down statistically into such components as pietism or ritualism. Similarly those reform movements that exposed social tensions such as the abolition of slavery, prohibition, and women's rights have been examined statistically by region, income, occupation, morbidity, fertility, and the like.

Nativism, which flourished during the massive immigration movements that began in the late 1840s and gained impetus during the 1850s, has also become the subject of intense study and is regarded by some historians as a prime political motivation to people living during this period. The "new" political historians follow the path that Lee Benson staked out in his study of the Jacksonians that was published in the early 1950s. With their concentration on local culture and on basic values that were either locally inspired or locally accepted, their work differs from all major schools of historical writing on the causes of the Civil War.

Joel Silbey and Michael Holt are currently the most prominent historians of the "new" political history. Silbey's essays, especially his article "The Civil War Synthesis" in *Civil War*

History 10 (1964), but also those he published in his volume *The Partisan Imperative* (New York, 1985), have sought to move historians away from slavery and sectionalism as prime causes for the conflict. Silbey argues that the masses north and south were influenced primarily by local concerns or prejudices. Elite groups engaged in issue-oriented politics that he feels brought on the conflict. Holt too in his studies *Forging a Majority: The Formation of the Republican Party in Pittsburgh, 1848–1860* (New York, 1969) and *The Political Crisis of the 1850's* (New York, 1978) has shown the impressive local appeal of nativism during the immediate prewar period. National issues like the slavery debate, public policy on tariffs and transportation, in short the entire spectrum of divisive issues that separated the sections have little or no place in his work or in that of Silbey for that matter.

A recent encyclopedic work on the creation of the Republican party also emphasizes the important role of nativism in forming that political coalition in 1856. William Gienapp's *The Origins of the Republican Party, 1850–1856* (New York, 1987) is in many respects the most convincing example of the "new" political history in the ethnocultural mold. Although his methodology seems at times to govern his conclusions (an overemphasis on nativism), Gienapp's mastery of quantitative techniques and his blending of these with data gleaned from traditional sources is truly remarkable. Yet Gienapp and other "new" political historians have not provided us with an overarching thesis that explains why the war came about. They have, however, supplied historians of the antebellum period with additional data of a significant nature and have perhaps shifted the current emphasis on "irrepressible conflict" to a deeper and fruitful investigation of mass social behavior.

Despite the arguments the "new" political and social historians have advanced, the study of slavery and race in antebellum society continues to provide most interesting and provocative debate. Don E. Fehrenbacher makes this point eloquently in his *Lincoln in Text and Context: Collected Essays* (Stanford, Calif., 1987).

Debate on Slavery and Race

In the mid-1950s Kenneth M. Stampp challenged the dominant Phillips thesis on slavery in *The Peculiar Institution* (New York, 1956). After exhaustive research in plantation records, he argued that slavery was highly profitable and that the picture that Phillips drew of blacks was completely distorted. Stampp argued moreover that blacks resisted slavery and constantly sought to sabotage the institution. Stanley Elkins, whose work came after Stampp's, in a way agreed with Phillips that the patriarchal system of slavery socialized the bondsmen, but his provocative book *Slavery, A Problem in American Institutional and Intellectual Life*, 3d ed. (Chicago, 1976), emphatically condemned the institution. Drawing on the concepts of Sigmund Freud and on Harry Stack Sullivan's theory of interpersonal relations, Elkins saw the slave as conditioned by a concentration camp mentality deliberately fostered by southern plantation owners. Although there were exceptions, of course, slaves usually became "Sambos" or human automatons. Elkins is also in substantial agreement with Frank Tannenbaum, who determined, in his pioneer study of comparative slavery *Slave and Citizen: the Negro in the Americas* (New York, 1947), that Spanish policy and the teachings of the Roman Catholic Church had made for a less rigorous institution of slavery than that found in the United States with its democratic state and its essentially Calvinist, Protestant culture.

As a result of these seminal works and the civil rights' agitation of the late 1950s and 1960s, race and slavery became popular topics for American historians. Eugene Genovese, while disputing Stampp's contention about the profitability of slavery and Elkin's "Sambo" model, emphasized the vigor and durability of Afro-American culture under the most difficult of circumstances. His thesis in *Roll, Jordan, Roll: The World the Slaves Made* (New York, 1974) centered on the contribution of blacks to southern and eventually to all of American culture. An earlier work of his that considers some of these themes is *The World the Slaveholders Made: Two Essays in*

Interpretation (New York, 1969). Although disagreeing on many points with Genovese, Herbert G. Gutman emphasized the solidity of the black family despite slavery. In his *Black Family in Slavery and Freedom, 1750–1920* (New York, 1976) Gutman took firm issue with Phillips and with Elkins. Carl N. Degler in his *Neither Black nor White: Slavery and Race Relations in Brazil and the United States* (New York, 1971) compared Brazilian slavery with North American. He pointed out the absence of a color barrier in Brazil but at the same time emphasized that the exploitation of the slave labor force in both cultures made it an atrocious form of human servitude. Bertram Wyatt-Brown, a thoughtful analyzer of modern works on slavery and blacks has seen a movement away from studying the social pathology of human slavery and a concentration on the tenacity of the bondsmen in preserving their cultural and social values despite the most adverse circumstances. Wyatt-Brown's collection of essays, *Northern Saints and Southern Sinners* (Baton Rouge, 1985), emphasizes this point among others. John Hope Franklin drew together many of these themes in the fifth edition of his fine study *From Slavery to Freedom: A History of Negro Americans* (New York, 1979).

It seemed that the following points regarding slavery and race were largely settled: (1) slavery was profitable, (2) black culture with its African roots became a vital aspect of the American heritage, (3) the black family was an integral unit at least until black ghetto conditions arose in American cities during the past seventy years. But in 1974 two economic historians, Robert W. Fogel and Stanley Engerman, published their controversial book *Time on the Cross*, 2 vols. (Boston, 1974). With a wealth of statistical data, they concentrated their attack on Stampp and on others they claimed were "impressionist" historians who lacked the mathematical expertise to evaluate hard data. Although their findings substantiated Stampp's on the profitability of slavery, they looked at the institution simply as a labor system that gained much more productivity from rewards rather than from punishments. They argued that slaves could not only rise in the system to responsible jobs that provided material gains, but that they received a greater share of the product from their labor than their free white counterparts in the north. In advocating what was dubbed the "Slave Horatio Alger" thesis, Fogel and Engerman were promptly attacked by the "impressionists" and by economic historians as well. Gutman, for instance, took up an entire issue of the *Journal of Negro History* for his rebuttal "The World Two Cliometricians Made: A Review Essay of F & E = T/c," (1975). Paul A. David, Herbert G. Gutman, Richard Such, Peter Temin, and Gavin Wright challenged the sources and the statistical analysis of *Time on the Cross* in *Reckoning with Slavery: A Critical Study in the Quantitative History of American Negro Slavery* (New York, 1976). Stampp ably defended himself in this collection. His essay entitled "A Humanistic Perspective" noted the preoccupation of Fogel and Engerman with efficiency at the expense of the human traits of "irrationality, friction, and conflict." And so the matter rests for the moment with the balance of the argument going to those opposed to the explanations in *Time on the Cross.*

On racism in the North and the plight of the free blacks in the South, two outstanding works are Leon F. Litwack, *North of Slavery: The Negro in The Free States, 1790–1860* (Chicago, 1961), and Ira Berlin, *Slaves Without Masters: The Free Negro in the Antebellum South* (New York, 1974). The use of slaves as members of the factory working force in the South is traced by Robert Starobin, *Industrial Slavery* (New York, 1970). For a discussion of slavery in the urban South, Richard C. Wade's *Slavery in the Cities* (New York, 1964) remains the best treatment of the subject. Specific abolitionists are treated well by Gerda Lerner, *The Grimké Sisters from South Carolina: Rebels against Slavery* (Boston, 1967), and Bertram Wyatt-Brown, *Lewis Tappan and the Evangelical War Against Slavery* (Cleveland, 1969).

The following are all excellent works on slavery and are recommended reading. The debate on slavery and the slave trade in the Constitutional convention of 1787 is in volume 2 of Max Farrand, ed. *The Records of the Federal Convention* of 1787, 4 vols. (New Haven, 1911). Other notable works are Philip D. Curtin, *The Atlantic Slave Trade* (Madison, Wisc., 1969); James A. Rawley, *The Transatlantic Slave Trade* (New York, 1981); David B. Davis, *The Problem of Slavery in the Age of Revolution, 1770–1823* (Ithaca, 1975); Nathan Huggins, *Black Odyssey: The Afro-American Ordeal in Slavery* (New York, 1977); Winthrop D. Jordan, *White Over Black: American Attitudes Toward the Negro, 1550–1812* (Chapel Hill, 1968); Lawrence W. Levine, *Black Culture and Black Consciousness: Afro-American Folk Thought From Slavery to Freedom* (New York, 1977); Leslie Howard Owens, *This Species of Property: Slave Life and Culture in the Old South* (New York, 1976); Barbara Jeanne Fields, *Slavery and Freedom on the Middle Ground* (New Haven, 1985); Willie Lee Rose, *Slavery and Freedom* (New York, 1982); John W. Blassingame, *The Slave Community*, (New York, 1972). Some recent scholarship has uncovered the racist attitudes of many abolitionist reformers. Perhaps the most stimulating of this historical genre is George M. Fredrickson, *The Black Image in the White Mind* (New York, 1971). But one should also consult Aileen Kraditor, *Means and Ends in American Abolitionism* (New York, 1969), and James A. Rawley, *Race and Politics* (Philadelphia, 1969). Other interesting interpretations of the abolitionists are essays by David Herbert Donald in his *Lincoln Reconsidered: Essays on the Civil War Era* (New York, 1956). See also Martin Duberman, *The Antislavery Vanguard: New Essays on the Abolitionists* (Princeton, 1965); James Russell Lowell (Boston, 1966); Louis Filler, *The Crusade Against Slavery, 1830–1860* (New York, 1972); George M. Fredrickson, *The Inner Civil War: Northern Intellectuals and the Crisis of the Union* (New York, 1965); and Russell B. Nye, *Fettered Freedom* (East Lansing, Mich., 1949). See as well Betty Fladeland, *James Gillespie Birney: Slaveholder to Abolitionist* (Ithaca, NY, 1955); Bertram Wyatt-Brown, *Lewis Tappan and the Evangelical War Against Slavery* (Cleveland, 1969); Lawrence J. Friedman, *Gregarious Saints: Self and Community in American Abolitionism, 1830–1870* (New York, 1985); Gilbert H. Barnes, *The Anti-Slavery*

Impulse, 1830–1844 (reprinted, Gloucester, Mass., 1973); James B. Stewart, *Joshua R. Giddings and the Tactics of Radical Politics* (Cleveland, 1970); and Ronald G. Walters, *The Antislavery Appeal* (Baltimore, 1976).

Events and Personalities

The literature on specific personalities and events that concern the coming of the Civil War is rich and varied. It is also highly contentious, involving as it does the roots of a conflict which historians have found especially hard to evaluate. Yet this great human tragedy in which more than 500,000 young men died and which devasted an entire region of the nation was the key event of American history during the nineteenth century. The sectional crisis that eventually resulted in the attack on Fort Sumter began with the deceptive calm of the Van Buren administration (1837–1841). These years were largely an extension of the Jacksonian age, a time when financial panic and deepening depression absorbed the energies of opinion leaders. But reform was in the air and an antislavery movement was gaining ground in the North, while countervailing actions were being prepared in the South.

Because the sectional conflict was muted until 1848, historians who have dealt in sweeping terms with the coming of the Civil War have tended to begin their studies with the Mexican-American War and the huge territorial cession that came as a result of the peace treaty. The annexation of Texas and the acquisition of California and the New Mexico Territory precipitated anew the debate over whether the republic would continue to tolerate the institution of slavery within its borders.

The historical literature that covers the years between Van Buren's inauguration and the advent of the Polk administration is characterized by special treatments in monographs and in biographies, though Robert H. Wiebe's *The Opening of American Society: From the Adoption of the Constitution to the Eve of Disunion* (New York, 1984) is an interesting overview of the cultural and social crosscurrents in the period. For a personal perspective, one should consult the wonderful journal of that Washington, D.C. insider, Benjamin Brown French. The journal, expertly edited by Donald B. Cole and John J. McDonough, is entitled *Witness to the Young Republic: A Yankee's Journal, 1828–1870* (Hanover, N.H., 1989). It illuminates the political and social life of the nation's capital before, during, and after the Civil War. For the Van Buren administration, Major Wilson's *The Presidency of Martin Van Buren* (Lawrence, Kan., 1984) is quite comprehensive. But it should be supplemented with James C. Curtis, *The Fox at Bay: Martin Van Buren and the Presidency* (Lexington, Ky., 1970); Donald B. Cole, *Martin Van Buren* (Princeton, 1984); John Niven, *Martin Van Buren: The Romantic Era of American Politics* (New York, 1983); Robert V. Remini, *Andrew Jackson and the Course of American Democracy, 1833–1845* (New York, 1984), vol. 3 of his marvelous biography of Andrew Jackson, and his *Martin Van Buren and the Making of the Democratic Party* (New York, 1959). Biographies of other leading figures contain much useful information on the growing sectional conflict until the temporary armistice of 1850. Charles M. Wiltse, *John C. Calhoun, Sectionalist, 1840–1850* (Indianapolis, 1951), volume 3 of the justly praised biography of this great defender of the Old South, is a valuable source, though Wiltse is too partial to Calhoun, as is Margaret L. Coit, *John C. Calhoun, American Portrait* (Boston, 1950). Gerald M. Capers, *John C. Calhoun, Opportunist: A Reappraisal* (Gainesville, Fla., 1960), offers a useful corrective, but see also John Niven, *John C. Calhoun and the Price of Union* (Baton Rouge, 1988). Daniel Webster and Henry Clay, who shared political leadership with Calhoun, are the subjects of a searching analysis by Merrill Peterson, *The Great Triumvirate: Webster, Clay, and Calhoun* (New York, 1987). Maurice G. Baxter, *One and Inseparable: Daniel Webster and the Union* (Cambridge, 1984), supplants all previous biographies. Glyndon Van Deusen, *The Life of Henry Clay* (Boston, 1937), is still the best one-volume treatment of the Kentucky statesman. It can be supplemented, however, with Clement Eaton's brief but interesting study *Henry Clay and the Art of American Politics* (Boston, 1957). Charles G. Sellers, *James K. Polk, Jacksonian, 1795–1843* (Princeton, 1957), and *James K. Polk, Continentalist, 1843–1846* (Princeton, 1966) are fine studies of border-state politics during the period and are equally valuable on the campaign and election of 1844. Apart from these volumes, the Harrison and Tyler administrations have been somewhat neglected. Robert G. Gunderson's *Log Cabin Campaign* (Lexington, Ky., 1957) is a notable account of what might be termed proto-modern presidential campaign practices. Robert J. Morgan has a sound treatment of Tyler in his *A Whig Embattled: The Presidency under John Tyler* (Lincoln, Neb., 1954).

There is no in-depth modern analysis of the Polk administration though the literature on the Mexican-American War and the diplomacy of the period is rich and abundant. Charles G. Sellers, *James K. Polk, Continentalist, 1843–1846* (Princeton, 1966), is excellent for the political break between Polk and Van Buren. But for the latter part of Polk's presidency, it is necessary to consult other sources. Two studies are suggested: Charles A. McCoy, *Polk and the Presidency* (Austin, 1960), and more recently, Paul H. Bergeron, *The Presidency of James K. Polk* (Lawrence, Kan., 1987). Polk's diary is a basic source. See Milo M. Quaife, ed. *The Diary of James K. Polk*, 4 vols. (Chicago, 1910), and also Allan Nevins, ed. *Diary of a President* (New York, 1929). Robert W. Johannsen, *To the Halls of Montezuma* (New York, 1985), is a splendid account of the Mexican-American War's impact on American society. Several important works deal with the expansionist impulse that saw a partial fulfillment in the Mexican-American War. They are: Frederick Merk, *Manifest Destiny and Mission in American History* (New York, 1963); Frederick Merk and Lois B. Merk, *The Monroe Doctrine and American Expansionism, 1843–1849* (New York, 1966); Albert K. Weinberg, *Manifest Destiny* (Baltimore, 1935); Dexter Perkins, *The Mon-*

roe Doctrine, 1826-1867 (Baltimore, 1933); and Norman A. Graebner, Empire on the Pacific (New York, 1955).

For the Whig party see Arthur Cole's venerable but still useful The Whig Party in the South (Washington, D.C., 1913), and his The Irrepressible Conflict, 1850-1865 (New York, 1934). Daniel Walker Howe, The Political Culture of the American Whigs (Chicago, 1979) is a stimulating study; Major Wilson has an interesting comparison of Whig and Jacksonian Democrat aims in his Space, Time, and Freedom: The Quest for Nationality and the Irrepressible Conflict, 1815-1861 (Westport, Conn., 1974). Glyndon Van Deusen's biographies of four Whig leaders, The Life of Henry Clay (Boston, 1937), Horace Greeley: Nineteenth Century Crusader (New York, 1953), Thurlow Weed, Wizard of the Lobby (New York, 1947), and William Henry Seward (New York, 1967) are all useful adjuncts to understanding the rise and fall of the Whig party. And in this category, Ronald P. Formisano's studies of Michigan and Massachusetts, The Birth of Mass Political Parties: Michigan, 1827-1861 (Princeton, 1971); The Transformation of Political Culture: Massachusetts Parties, 1790s-1840s (New York, 1983), are solid examples of the "new" political history. Marvin Meyers, The Jacksonian Persuasion: Politics and Belief (Stanford, 1957), is a classic statement of Jacksonian rhetoric and belief. Joel Silbey, a "new" political historian, has done useful work on the origins and organization of the second American party system. See especially The Shrine of Party: Congressional Voting Behavior, 1841-1852 (Pittsburgh, 1967), Political Ideology and Voting Behavior in the Age of Jackson (Englewood Cliffs, N.J., 1973), and The Partisan Imperative (New York, 1985). Chaplain Morrison has a full and interesting account of the Wilmot Proviso in his Democratic Politics and Sectionalism: The Wilmot Proviso Controversy (Chapel Hill, N.C., 1967). The Free Soil campaign has claimed some attention. See Frederick J. Blue, The Free Soilers: Third Party Politics, 1848-54 (Urbana, 1973); Joseph Rayback, Free Soil: The Election of 1848 (Lexington, Ky., 1970).

The Taylor and Fillmore administrations are well covered

in three biographies: Holman Hamilton, *Zachary Taylor*, 2 vol. (Indianapolis, 1941; New York, 1951); K. Jack Bauer, *Zachary Taylor* (Lawrence, Kan., 1986); Robert J. Rayback, *Millard Fillmore* (Buffalo, 1959). Holman Hamilton, *Prologue to Conflict: The Crisis and Compromise of 1850* (Lexington, Ky., 1964), is the best one-volume treatment of the Compromise. But it must be supplemented by Robert Johannsen's masterful biography, *Stephen A. Douglas* (New York, 1972). Roy F. Nichols, *Democratic Machine* (New York, 1923); *Franklin Pierce, Young Hickory From the Granite Hills* (Philadelphia, 1958); *Stakes of Power* (New York, 1961), all deal specifically with Democratic party politics during the Pierce administration. The Kansas problem is expertly developed in Johannsen's *Douglas* and also in Don Fehrenbacher, *Prelude to Greatness: Lincoln in the 1850's* (Stanford, 1962); James C. Malin, *The Nebraska Question* (Lawrence, Kan., 1953); Alice Nichols, *Bleeding Kansas* (New York, 1954); James A. Rawley, *Race and Politics* (New York, 1969); David Herbert Donald, *Charles Sumner and the Coming of the Civil War* (New York, 1960); Roy F. Nichols, *Disruption of American Democracy* (New York, 1958); and Philip S. Klein, *President James Buchanan* (University Park, Pa., 1962). Early chapters of Hans L. Trefousse's admirable *Andrew Johnson, A Biography* (New York, 1989) are well worth studying.

The formation of the Republican party has attracted a good deal of historical interest. Michael F. Holt and William Gienapp have studied the origins of the Republican coalition from an ethnocultural basis. But one should also consult Robert Kelly's *The Transatlantic Persuasion: The Liberal Democratic Mind in the Age of Gladstone*, (New York, 1969), which sees a distinct link between ethnocultural unrest caused by modernization in England and the United States. As such it should be balanced against Eric Foner, *Free Soil, Free Labor, Free Men* (New York, 1970); Fred H. Harrington, *Fighting Politician: Major General N. P. Banks* (Philadelphia, 1948); John Niven, *Gideon Welles, Lincoln's Secretary of the Navy;* (New York, 1973) Allan Nevins, *Emergence of Lincoln*, 2 vol.

(New York, 1950), and David M. Potter, *The Impending Crisis* (New York, 1976). In fact, Potter's *Impending Crisis* and Nevins's *Ordeal of the Union* and *Emergence of Lincoln* are masterworks that are indispensable to a study of the entire period. Mention should also be made of Charles Sydnor, *The Development of Southern Sectionalism* (Baton Rouge, 1948); Avery Craven, *The Coming of the Civil War* (New York, 1942), and *The Growth of Southern Nationalism, 1848–1861* (Baton Rouge, 1953); William J. Cooper, *The South and the Politics of Slavery, 1828–1856* (Baton Rouge, 1978), the insightful essays of Kenneth M. Stampp in his *The Imperiled Union* (New York, 1980) and Drew Gilpin Faust's fine biography *James Henry Hammond* (Baton Rouge, 1982). Another overview of the period that emphasizes sectional conflict and other profound differences between the North and the South is Richard Sewell's *A House Divided: Sectionalism and the Civil War* (Baltimore, 1988). For a comparison of southern and northern cultures during the antebellum period, William R. Taylor, *Cavalier and Yankee: The Old South and American National Character* (New York, 1961) is still the most provocative treatment of this elusive topic. But see also Bertram Wyatt-Brown, *Southern Honor: Ethics and Behavior in the Old South* (New York, 1982) and W. J. Cash, *The Mind of the South* (New York, 1941). There are also stimulating essays on the antebellum South in Arthur S. Link and Rembert W. Patrick, *Writing Southern History: Essays in Historiography in Honor of Fletcher M. Green* (Baton Rouge, 1965); and Robert F. Durden, *The Self-Inflicted Wound: Southern Politics in the Nineteenth Century* (Lexington, Ky., 1985), has several chapters that deal in a broad way with southern antebellum politics.

The best book on the Dred Scott decision is Don E. Fehrenbacher's *The Dred Scott Case* (New York, 1978); but Paul Finkleman's *An Imperfect Union: Slavery, Federalism and Comity* (Chapel Hill, 1981) is also well worth studying. Walter Ehrlich has a brief though interesting account of the background of the case in his "The Origins of the Dred Scott Case,"

Journal of Negro History 59 (1972): 132–142. The most stimulating economic history of the period is still Douglass C. North, *Economic Growth of the United States, 1790–1860* (New York, 1966). And George R. Taylor, *The Transportation Revolution, 1815–1860* (New York, 1951) remains the most comprehensive history of transportation for the period. But Gavin Wright's *The Political Economy of the Cotton South: Households, Markets, and Wealth in the Nineteenth Century* (New York, 1978) deals more specifically with the one-crop slave-plantation system. Also of value is Harold D. Woodman, *King Cotton and His Retainers: Financing and Marketing the Cotton Crop of the South, 1800–1925* (Lexington, Ky., 1968). Raimondo Luraghi has written an interesting article on modernization from a European standpoint entitled "The Civil War and the Modernization of American Society: Social Structure and Industrial Revolution in the Old South Before and During the War" *Civil War History* 18 (1972). Four general works treat modernization in a comprehensive manner. They are C. E. Black, *The Dynamics of Modernization* (New York, 1966); James McPherson's stimulating textbook on the war, *Ordeal by Fire* (New York, 1982) and his acclaimed *Battle Cry of Freedom* (New York, 1988); and Richard D. Brown, *Modernization* (New York, 1976). For innovative discussions of the secession movement see Michael Johnson, *Towards a Patriarchal Republic: The Secession of Georgia* (Baton Rouge, 1977); and Steven A. Channing, *Crisis of Fear: Secession in South Carolina* (New York, 1970). Two other recent works are recommended: William L. Barney, *The Secessionist Impulses: Alabama and Mississippi in 1860* (Princeton, 1974), and Lacy K. Ford's interesting study of tensions in South Carolina entitled *The Origins of Southern Radicalism: The South Carolina Upcountry, 1800–1860* (New York, 1988).

A compelling account of the Lincoln-Douglas debates is to be found in Potter's *Impending Crisis*. But Johannsen's *Douglas*, Nevins's *Emergence of Lincoln*, volume 1, and Harry Jaffa's *Crisis of the House Divided: An Interpretation of the Issues in the Lincoln-Douglas Debates*, (Seattle, 1959), each makes a significant contribution to these historic arguments over slavery and free soil. Of the many biographies of Lincoln, James G. Randall's *Lincoln the Liberal Statesman* (New York, 1947) and volume 1 of his *Lincoln the President* (New York, 1945) are outstanding. Two one-volume biographies of Lincoln are also worthy of note: Benjamin Thomas, *Abraham Lincoln* (New York, 1952) and Stephen B. Oates, *With Malice Toward None: The Life of Abraham Lincoln* (New York, 1977), a modern revisionist interpretation of Lincoln. Another excellent volume that must be included in any analysis of Lincoln is Richard Current's *The Lincoln Nobody Knows* (New York, 1958).

The failure of compromise after the election of Lincoln has attracted considerable attention from historians who have debated Lincoln's role in the secession crisis and the eventual attack on Fort Sumter. Richard N. Current, *Lincoln and the First Shot* (Philadelphia, 1963); Allan Nevins, *War for the Union*, volume 1 (New York, 1959); John Niven, *Gideon Welles, Lincoln's Secretary of the Navy* (New York, 1973), Kenneth M. Stampp, *And the War Came* (Baton Rouge, 1950); David Potter, *Lincoln and His Party in the Secession Crisis* (rev. ed., New Haven, 1962), are in general agreement that Lincoln did not at first appreciate the extreme gravity of the situation. They differ, however, over his responsibility for forcing the issue at Sumter.

Special topics that contribute in one way or another to an understanding of the coming of the Civil War—abolitionism, feminist history, and changing interpretations of slavery and race—have been studied intensively over the past thirty years. On the broad subject of antebellum reform in the United States, Ronald Walters, *American Reformers, 1815–1860* (New York, 1978) is both comprehensive and stimulating. It replaces the familiar yet still useful book by Alice Felt Tyler, *Freedom's Ferment* (Minneapolis, 1944). For the abolition movement as a whole, the best book is James Brewer Stewart, *Holy Warriors: The Abolitionists and American Slavery* (New York, 1976). But Lewis Perry, *Radical Abolitionism: Anarchy and the Government of God in Anti-Slavery Thought (Ithaca, New York, 1973), presents an insightful interpretation of the intellectual background of the abolitionist movement. Benjamin Quarles, Black Abolitionists (New York, 1969), is especially useful for the interaction between white and black abolitionist leaders. Richard H. Sewell has written the best treatment of abolitionist political action in Ballots for Freedom: Antislavery Politics in the United States, 1837–1860 (New York, 1976) and in John P. Hale and the Politics of Abolition (Cambridge, 1965).

The history of women and of the family have also claimed major attention. The most thoughtful of these works are: Nancy F. Cott, The Bonds of Womanhood (New Haven, 1977); Anne Douglas, The Feminization of American Culture (New York, 1977); Eleanor Flexner, Century of Struggle: The Woman's Rights Movement in the United States (Rev. ed, Cambridge, 1975); Mary Kelley, Private Woman, Public Stage (New York, 1984); Barbara Welter, Dimity Convictions: The American Woman in the Nineteenth Century (Athens, Ohio, 1976), and Carl Degler, At Odds: Women and the Family from the Revolution to the Present (New York, 1980).

Temperance and prohibition are best served in W. J. Rorabaugh, The Alcoholic Republic: An American Tradition (New York, 1979); and in Ian R. Tyrrell, Sobering Up: From Temperance to Prohibition in Antebellum America 1800–1860 (Westport, 1979).

In the broad area of southern studies, an interesting recent example of the "new" social history is the detailed analysis of Edgefield County, South Carolina by Orville Vernon Burton entitled In My Father's House Are Many Mansions (Chapel Hill, N.C., 1985). But one should also consult Carl N. Degler, The Other South: Southern Dissenters in the Nineteenth Century (New York, 1974) as well as David Potter's The South and Sectional Conflict (Baton Rouge, 1948). Another recent contribution is Elizabeth Fox-Genovese's Within the Plantation Household: Black and White Women in the Old South (Chapel Hill, N.C., 1988).

For the intellectual and literary history of the period, one should consult volume 2 of Vernon L. Parrington's *Main Currents in American Thought*, 3 vols. (New York, 1927); appropriate chapters from Merle Curti's *Growth of American Thought*, 3d ed. (New York, 1964); and Rush Welter, *The Mind of America, 1820–1860* (New York, 1975).

Historical explanations of the causes of conflict from the northern nationalism of contemporary observers like Henry Wilson and Herman von Holst through the revisionist views of the Dunning and Dodd schools, the southern nationalism of a Ramsdell or an Owsley, the liberal, northern interpretations of Arthur Schlesinger, Jr., and Oscar Handlin, the attempts of both Nevins and Potter to provide a synthesis, and finally the efforts of the "new" political and social historians to emphasize the role of local pressures and the response of the average citizen to these developments have all shown how interpretations of historians have changed over time and have responded to the particular social and cultural environments in which they have worked.

It is not possible to escape the fact that the Civil War did come and that it lasted for four years. It cost the lives of more than a half million young Americans and over five billion dollars in 1865 terms, perhaps one hundred billion dollars in 1989 terms. Was it necessary to pay this price for emancipation? Could not slavery, which even in 1861 had become an anachronism and had always in modern times been considered a moral and social abomination, been eradicated if leading figures north and south had thought soberly what war would mean and had taken steps to prevent it? Historians, it seems, are as unable as the actual participants in those events to provide an answer. Yet as E. H. Carr, the famed British historian of modern Russia, has said, "objectivity in history—if we are still to use the conventional term—cannot be an objectivity of fact, but only of relations between fact and interpretation between past, present, and future." It is entirely possible that the complex forces and events that created the Civil War will be re-evaluated in a more meaningful way at some point in the future. Current interpretations may well be replaced by the ideas and insights of another generation, another audience that asks a different set of questions.

INDEX

Abolitionists, 19–23, 32–34, 38, 39, 45, 83; black, 40, 41, 49, 113
Adams, Charles Francis, 86, 133
Adams, Henry, 1, 16
Adams, John Quincy, 15, 98; and right of petition, 19, 20, 49; on internal improvements, 75
Aiken, William, 92
Alabama, 75
Albany Regency, 30
American Revolution, 4, 5, 7, 51, 75
"American System," 32, 47, 75
Anderson, Major Robert, 132, 140, 141
"Appeal to Independent Democrats," 82, 83
Arizona, state of, 52
Ashburton, Lord, 48
Astor, John Jacob, 50
Atchison, David R., 88, 89, 91, 104

Baltimore, Md., 31, 124, 136, 138, 142
Bancroft, Frederic, 9
Bancroft, George, 52
Banks, Nathaniel P., 86, 92, 96, 116
"Barnburners," 52, 56, 73
Bates, Edward, 125, 137
Bayard, James A., 123
Beecher, Henry Ward, 38, 126
Bell, John, 124, 129

Benton, Thomas H., 76, 77
Bigler, William, 123
Big Springs, Kan., 90
Birney, James G., 36, 37, 51
Black, Jeremiah S., 132
Beauregard, P. G. T., 140, 141
Black Warrior, 84
Blacks, as slaves, 2, 3; Jim Crow Laws, 40; colonization of, 8, 40, 85; and Dred Scott case, 101, 102; and Lincoln-Douglas debates, 111, 112
Blair, Francis P., 86, 100
Blair, Francis P., Jr., 86
Blair, Montgomery, 86, 100, 139
Border slave states, 135, 138, 139; division of, 142
Boston, Mass., 23, 34
Breckinridge, John C., 98, 124; and election of 1860, 129
Bright, Jesse, 55, 123
Brougham, Henry, 36
Brooks, Preston, 94
Brown, John, xiv, 93, 94; raid on Harpers Ferry, 113, 114, 116, 127; execution of, 115
Bryant, William Cullen, 87, 126
Buchanan, James, xiii, xiv, 35, 51, 53, 73, 84, 97–99, 101, 103, 104, 106–109, 115, 116, 123, 132
Burleigh, Charles C., 33
Bushnell, Horace, 12

Butler, Andrew, 94

Calhoun, John C., xiii, 29, 35, 51, 53, 56, 58, 62; despairs of Union, 16, 20; and Texas, 22; and tariff policy, 26, 27, 36, 37; secretary of state, 48, 49; and compromise of 1850, 59, 60, 65, 66; on internal improvements, 75, 117, 122
California, xiii, 52, 53, 54, 55, 58–61, 64, 69, 72
Cameron, Simon, 137
Canada, 45, 48
Cartwright, Peter, 43
Cass, Lewis, 55–57, 73, 82, 97, 132
Catron, John, 101
Charleston, S.C., ix, 88, 123, 132
Chase, Salmon P., 6, 40, 41, 57, 82, 86, 87, 97, 103, 110, 124–125; secretary of treasury, 137
Channing, William Ellery, 33
Chesnut, James, Jr., 35
Chesnut, Mary Boykin, 35
Chevalier, Michel, quoted, 25
"Christian stewardship," 38
Clarkson, Thomas, 14, 36
Clay, Clement C., 134
Clay, Henry, 22, 23, 28, 31, 32, 41, 46, 56, 98; and Texas, 49, 50, 51; and Compromise of 1850, 59, 60; on internal improvements, 75, 76
Clayton, John M., 55
Cobb, Howell, 35, 79, 130–131, 132
Colonies, American, contrasts between, 3, 4
Colorado, state of, 53
Compromise of 1850, xiii, 15, 60, 64, 66, 70, 73, 74, 79, 80, 100
Confederate States of America, xiv, 16; provisional, 131, 135, 138, 139
Connecticut, state of, 86
Constitution, federal, fugitive slave clause in, 7
Conventions
    Nashville, xiii, 61
    Philadelphia 1787, 1, 5; 1856, 97
    Harrisburg, 30, 31
    Seneca Falls, 38

Baltimore, 1860, 124
Pittsburgh, 86
Charleston, xiv, 117, 123, 124
Cincinnati, 97
Chicago, 127
Cooper Union, 126
Cotton economy, 28, 63, 64, 69–71, 116, 118
Cotton gin, 8, 9
Covode, John, 116
Crimean War, 72, 96
Crittenden Compromise, 133
"Cult of domesticity," 37
Curtis, Benjamin R., 100–102

Davis, Jefferson, 16, 74, 78, 81, 95, 116, 117, 134, 213; elected President, Provisional Confederacy, 131, 141, 147
Dayton, William, 97
Declaration of Independence, 7, 38, 65, 109
Deposit Banking Act, 19
Depression of 1857, 72, 115, 116
Dickinson, Daniel, 55
Dickens, Charles, 13
Distribution, 47
Dix, John A., 132
Donelson, Andrew J., 96
"Doughfaces," 91
Douglas, Stephen A., xiii, 54, 70, 73; and compromise of 1850, 60, 61; on territories, 71, 77–81; and Kansas-Nebraska Act, 79–84, 85, 86, 94, 97, 102, 103, 105, 106, 107; debates Lincoln, 110–112, 115, 116, 117, 121–123; and election of 1860, 129, 130, 146
Douglass, Frederick, 39–42
Dow, Neal, 42
Dred Scott case, xiii, 57, 99–105
Duke of Sussex, 36

English, William H., 108
Erie Canal, 78
Evans, George Henry, 26
Everett, Edward, 124

"Father" Lampson, 33

Filibustering expeditions, 73, 84
Fillmore, Millard, 61, 73, 96, 97
Financial panics, 1837, xiii, 28; 1857, 116
Finney, Charles Grandison, 38, 43
Fitzpatrick, Benjamin, 124, 134
Florida, state of, 21; purchase of, 76
Floyd, John, 132
Foote, Henry S., 108
Fort Johnson, 141
Fort Pickens, 136, 139, 140
Fort Snelling, 99
Fort Sumter, xiv, 17, 129, 132, 140; surrenders, 141
Foster, Abby Kelley, 38
Fox, Gustavus Vasa, 139–141
Free Soil, 15, 54, 55, 89, 91, 92, 105
Frémont, John C., xiii, 97–99
Freeport Doctrine, 111
Fugitive Slave Act of 1793, 7; of 1850, 60–62, 74, 122; Constitutional clause, 55, 62

Gadsden Purchase, xiii, 53, 78
Garnet, Henry Highland, 41
Garrison, William Lloyd, 20, 33, 39
Geary, John W., 104, 105
German states, 21
Georgia, state of, 5, 10, 33
Geyer, Henry S., 100
Giddings, Joshua, 82, 83
Gilmer, Thomas W., 48
Great Britain, 8, 9, 32, 45, 53, 64; modernization in, 13; opposition to slavery, 21, 39
Greeley, Horace, 24, 42, 46, 87, 125, 126, 146
Grier, Robert C., 101
Grimké, Angelina, 38
Grimké, Sarah, 38
Guizot, François, 36

Hale, John P., 57, 74
Hamilton, Alexander, 2, 122
Hamlin, Hannibal, 128, 137
Hammond, James Henry, 35, 63, 116
Harpers Ferry, xiv, 113–116
Harrisburg, Pa., 31, 136

Harrison, W. H., xiii, 31, 36–38, 46, 47, 48
Helper, Hinton, 118
Herndon, Billy, 125
Holt, Joseph, 132
Hone, Philip, 28
Houston, Sam, 22
"Hunkers," 52, 55, 56, 73
Hutchinson family, 33

Illinois Central Railroad, 77
Illinois, state of, 36, 60, 70, 85, 101, 109
Immigration, 69, 70
Internal improvements, 32, 47, 75
Iowa, state of, 21
"Irrepressible Conflict," 13, 17, 124

Jackson, Andrew, 18, 19, 21, 47, 96; on Texas, 22
Jefferson, Thomas, 2, 6, 7, 47, 53, 122
Johnson, Andrew, 77
Johnson, Herschel V., 124
Johnson, Reverdy, 100
Johnston, William P., 96

Kansas-Nebraska Act, xiii, 79–84, 89, 98, 100, 102, 115
Kansas, territory of, 87–92, 97, 99, 104–109, 118
Kentucky, state of, 74, 142
King, Preston, 86
King, T. Butler, 59

Labor, 26, 30
Lane, Joseph, 124
Lane, James "Jim," 91
Lawrence, Kan, 90, 93
Lecompte, Samuel D., 88
Lecompton constitution, xiii, 106–109
Liberia, 41
Lemmon v. People, 103
Lincoln, Abraham, 1, 6, 86, 103, 135, 136; on nature of Union, 16, 41, 77; Peoria speech, 85; challenges Douglas, 109; debates,

110–112; "House Divided" speech, 125; Cooper Union address, 126, 127; Republican nomination, 128; and election of 1860, 129, 130; Crittenden Compromise, 133; cabinet appointments, 137; border state policy, 138, 139, 140
Lincoln-Douglas debates, xiii, 110–112
London, anti-slavery convention, 36
Louisiana, state of, 63, 75; purchase, 76, 79, 80
Louis Philippe, 25
Lower South, 7; and cotton culture, 8, 9; secedes from Union, 130, 131, 134, 135

McLean, John, 100–102
Madison, James, 1, 2, 122
Mallory, Stephen K., 134
"Manifest Destiny," 22, 51, 70
Maine Law, 42
Marbury v. Madison, 102
Marcy, William L., 52, 73, 81, 85
Marshall, John, 27, 62, 122
Martin, Luther, 6
Maryland, state of, 6, 135, 138, 142; railroads in, 10, 30, 39
Mason, George, 6
Mason, James M., 60, 84
Massachusetts Emigrant Aid Society, 87, 90
Massachusetts, state of, 1, 15, 39, 74, 86
May, Samuel, 20
Mellon, George W., 33
Memphis, Tenn., 78
Mexican-American War, 10, 15, 49, 53, 63, 64, 71–74, 76, 78, 121
Mexican Cession, 15, 53, 54, 66, 69, 76, 80
Mexico, xiii, 22, 49, 52
Mexico City, 52
Michigan, state of, 21
Minnesota, territory, 78, 99, 102
Mississippi River, 11, 75, 78
Mississippi, state of, 61, 75
Missouri Compromise, 8, 10, 54,

57, 61, 79–82, 88, 99–102, 122, 133
Missouri, state of, 10, 79, 93, 99, 101, 104
Middle Atlantic states, 4, 8
Modernization, 9, 64, 118, 142
Monroe, James, 31; Doctrine, 98
Morgan, Edmund, 3
Morgan, Edwin D., 121
Morgan, William, 30
Morse, Samuel F. B., 45
Mott, Lucretia, 38

National Banking Act, 29
Nativism, 15, 70
Nebraska Territory, 79
Nevada, state of, 53
New England, 8, 10, 12, 25, 30, 62, 113
Newspapers, 11, 24; black abolitionist, 40; antislavery, 82
New Mexico, state of, 52; territory of, 54, 55, 59, 60, 63, 78, 79, 80, 134
New Orleans, 78
New York City, 23, 24; pauperism in, 26
New York, state of, 33, 36, 51, 56, 73, 86, 113; factional conflicts in, 73
Nichols, Roy F., 12
Nicholson, A. O. P., 56
Niles, John M., 11, 49, 74, 86
North Carolina, state of, 138
Norfolk, Va. navy yard, 142
Northwest Ordinance, 10, 53, 57, 110
Nullification, 27, 47

O'Connell, Daniel, 36
Ohio Company, 76
Ohio, state of, 36, 86, 87; Black Laws of, 40
Old Gentleman's Convention, 135
"Omnibus bill," 60
Oregon Territory, 50, 51, 53–55, 64
Oklahoma, 53
Ostend Manifesto, xiii, 84–85
O'Sullivan, John L., 51

Owen, Robert, 13

Pakenham, Sir Richard, 49
Panics, 1837, xiii, 28; 1857, 116
Parker, Theodore, 38
Pennington, William, 116
Pennsylvania, state of, 36, 86
Peoria, Ill., 85
Personal Liberty Laws, 7, 62, 122
Philadelphia, 23, 24
Phillips, Wendell, 33, 42
Pierce, Franklin, xiii, 73, 74, 79, 81, 82, 83, 84, 87, 88, 90–93, 97, 104
Pickens, Francis, 63, 140
Pinckney, Charles, 6
Political parties: *Democratic*, xiii, xiv, 12, 14, 19, 46, 47, 48, 64, 65, 70, 71–73, 80–82, 84, 91, 92; and "Equal Rights," 23, 24; sectional differences in, 26, 29, 32, 34; and "popular sovereignty," 55, 56; election of 1852, 74; and internal improvements, 75; Free Soil, 85, 86; election of 1856, 98, 99; and Lecompton constitution, 106, 107, 112, 113, 116; and election of 1860, 117, 121, 124, 125, 128; *National Republican*, 31, 75; *Anti-Mason*, 30, 31; *Whig*, xiii, 12, 14–16, 46–48, 53, 64, 65, 72, 73, 84, 86; election of 1840, 36; of 1848, 56, 58; and Compromise of 1850, 11; free soil, 71, 85; election of 1852, 74, 80, 83; on Texas, 22, 29–32, 34; and internal improvements, 75; *Liberty*, xiii, 22, 23, 36, 51, 57; *Free Soil*, xiii, 16, 56, 57, 63, 64, 70, 74, 79, 107; *American (Know Nothing)*, 16, 86, 91, 92, 96, 98; *North American*, 96, 97; *South American*, 96, 97; *Republican*, xiii, 16, 63, 86, 87, 91, 96, 98, 99, 135; and Dred Scott decision, 103, 104, 112, 113, 116; and election of 1860, 117, 118, 121, 124, 125, 128, 129; and Crittenden Compromise, 133; *Constitutional Union*, 124, 125, 129

Polk, James K., xiii, 49–56, 58, 73, 77, 98, 105
Polk, Leonidas, 142
"Popular sovereignty": 56, 79, 80, 105, 106, 107, 117, 122, 123
Pottawatomie Creek, 93
Prigg v. Pennsylvania, 62, 63
Prohibition, 42
Pryor, Mrs. Roger, 35–36
Public land policy, 75–77; "preemption," 76; "graduation," 77; distribution, 77; homestead bills, 76, 77

Quincy, Edmund, 33

Railroads, 10; construction of, 11, 32, 35, 64, 69; transcontinental, 74, 75, 78
Reeder, Andrew H., 88–90, 92, 104
Reform movements, 13, 14, 32, 37, 43
Robinson, Charles, 90, 91, 93
Russell, William Howard, 12

St. Louis, 78
Saint-Simon, Claude, Comte de, 13
San Diego, Calif., 78
Sanford, John, 99
San Francisco, 52, 78
Scott, Winfield, xiii, 31, 52, 74, 136, 141
Secession, xiv, 61, 122, 130, 131
Sectionalism, 7, 22, 65, 74; modernization as factor in, 9, 15, 26; in Congress, 21
Seward, William H., 13, 17, 33, 59, 65, 71, 73, 86, 95, 97, 124–128, 136; Secretary of State, 137, 138, 141, 148
Shannon, Wilson, 90, 91, 93, 104
Shawnee Mission, Kan., 90, 92, 93
Sherman, John, 94, 145
Sherman, William Tecumseh, 145
Shields, James, 85
Slade, William, 19
Slavery, 2, 12, 20, 25, 48, 49, 54, 56, 60, 64, 66, 82, 83, 86; and

social stability, 3, 7, 117, 118;
abolition of, 14, 20, 32, 36;
petitions opposing, 15; churches
on, 15; as cause of Civil War, 16,
143; in District of Columbia, 18,
97; in Texas, 22; political
positions on, 32, 36; fugitives, 33,
34, 35, 40; and due process, 57;
proslavery conventions, 58; and
Kansas, 88, 91; and Lincoln-
Douglas debates, 110-112, 130,
142, 143

Slave trade, 5, 6; domestic, 9, 21;
abolition of in the D.C., 60, 74;
external, 14
Slidell, John, 52, 95, 123
Smith, Caleb, 137
Smith, Gerrit, 20, 82, 113
Soulé, Pierre, 84
South Carolina, state of, 5, 6, 7, 33,
61, 63; railroads in, 109, 122
"Specie Circular," 19
"Spoils system," 23
Stanton, Edwin M., 132
Stanton, Elizabeth Cady, 33
Stanton, Henry B., 33
Star of the West, 132
States' rights, 2, 22, 23, 29, 62, 63,
71, 122
Stephens, Alexander H., 131, 147
Story, Joseph, 62, 122
Stowe, Harriet Beecher, 82, 83
Stowe, Calvin, 38
Strong, George Templeton, 115, 122
Subtreasury system, 29, 72
Sumner, Charles, xiii, 63, 82, 86,
92, 94, 95

Taney, Roger B., 18, 100-103
Tariff, 26, 46, 48; of 1828, 27;
compromise, 27, 28, 47, 54;
Walker, 105, 115
Taylor, Zachary, xiii, 52, 56-58;
and Compromise of 1850, 60, 71
Telegraph, 11, 35
Tennessee, 74
Texas, xiii, Republic of, 21-22, 75;
annexation of, 48, 51, 52; state of,

53-55, 63; and compromise of
1850, 60
Thayer, Eli, 87, 88, 90
Thompson, Jacob, 132
Tocqueville, Alexis de, 25
Toombs, Robert, 80, 141
Topeka, Kan, 90; Constitution, 91-
93
Toucey, Isaac, 106, 107
Tyler, John, 22, 47, 48, 51; and
"Old Gentlemen's Convention,"
135
Treaties, 16; Guadalupe Hidalgo,
xiii, 53
Trist, Nicholas, 53
Trumbull, Lyman, 85

Uncle Tom's Cabin, xiii, 82
Upper South, 7; and colonization
movement, 8
Upshur, Abel P., 48
U.S.S. Powhatan, 140
Utah, state of, 53

Van Buren, Martin, xiii, 16, 19-20,
22, 26, 27, 42, 47, 51; inaugural
address of, 18, 19, 29; and Texas,
49, 50; and subtreasury, 29; Free
Soil candidate, 56; quoted, 56, 57,
74
Van Zandt case, 110
Vermont, 74
Virginia, cash crops in, 2; soil
exhaustion in, 6, 7, 30, 33, 75
Virginia and Kentucky resolutions,
27, 122

Wade, Edward, 83
Wade, Benjamin, 92
"Wakarusa War," 91
Walker, Robert J., 51, 105-106
War of 1812, 75, 76
Washington, D.C., 1, 12, 10, 35, 36,
54, 58, 90, 138
Washington, territory of, 50; state
of, 53
Webster, Daniel, 31, 46, 47, 56, 59,

60; and Compromise of 1850, 60, 71, 122
Weed, Thurlow, 31, 46, 73, 86, 124, 126, 138
Weld, Theodore Dwight, 38
Welles, Gideon, 10, 64–65, 108, 137, 146
Whittier, John G., 33
White, Hugh Lawson, 31
Whitney, Eli, 8
Wilberforce, William, 14

Wilmot Proviso, xiii, 49, 53, 55–58, 60, 64
Wilson, Henry, 92, 146
Wirt, William, 31
Wisconsin, state of, 21
Wise, Henry A., 20
Wyoming, state of, 53

Yancey, William Lowndes, 123, 130
"Young America," 70, 74
Yulee, David L., 134

The Coming of the Civil War, 1837–1861 was copyedited and proofread by J. Michael Kendrick. Production editor was Lucy Herz. Maps were prepared by James A. Bier. The text was typeset by Impressions, Inc., and printed and bound by Edwards Brothers, Inc.

The cover and text were designed by Roger Eggers.